ISBN 978-1-5277-1367-3
PIBN 10883521

This book is a reproduction of an important historical work. Forgotten Books uses
state-of-the-art technology to digitally reconstruct the work, preserving the original format
whilst repairing imperfections present in the aged copy. In rare cases, an imperfection in
the original, such as a blemish or missing page, may be replicated in our edition. We do,
however, repair the vast majority of imperfections successfully; any imperfections that
remain are intentionally left to preserve the state of such historical works.

1 MONTH OF
FREE
READING

at

www.ForgottenBooks.com

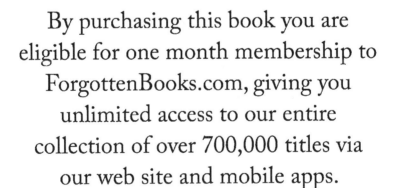

By purchasing this book you are eligible for one month membership to ForgottenBooks.com, giving you unlimited access to our entire collection of over 700,000 titles via our web site and mobile apps.

To claim your free month visit:
www.forgottenbooks.com/free883521

English
Français
Deutsche
Italiano
Español
Português

www.forgottenbooks.com

Mythology Photography **Fiction**
Fishing Christianity **Art** Cooking
Essays Buddhism Freemasonry
Medicine **Biology** Music **Ancient**
Egypt Evolution Carpentry Physics
Dance Geology **Mathematics** Fitness
Shakespeare **Folklore** Yoga Marketing
Confidence Immortality Biographies
Poetry **Psychology** Witchcraft
Electronics Chemistry History **Law**
Accounting **Philosophy** Anthropology
Alchemy Drama Quantum Mechanics
Atheism Sexual Health **Ancient History**
Entrepreneurship Languages Sport
Paleontology Needlework Islam
Metaphysics Investment Archaeology
Parenting Statistics Criminology
Motivational

LETTERS

OF

JOHN HUSS,

WRITTEN DURING HIS EXILE AND IMPRISONMENT;

WITH

MARTIN LUTHER'S PREFACE;

AND CONTAINING A

GENERAL VIEW OF THE WORKS OF HUSS.

BY

ÉMILE DE BONNECHOSE,

AUTHOR OF "THE REFORMERS BEFORE THE REFORMATION," ETC.

Translated by

CAMPBELL MACKENZIE, B.A.,

TRIN. COLL. DUBLIN.

EDINBURGH:
WILLIAM WHYTE & CO.,
BOOKSELLERS TO THE QUEEN DOWAGER;
LONDON: LONGMAN AND CO.; DUBLIN: W. CURRY JUN., AND CO.

MDCCCXLVI.

1848. Nov. 14

in exchange for Quizet, anto

PRINTED BY NEILL AND COMPANY, EDINBURGH.

CONTENTS.

SECOND SERIES.

NOTES.

INTRODUCTION.

TOWARDS the end of the fourteenth century there was born in Bohemia, a man whose name is inseparably connected with one of the most important revolutions of modern Europe. His history I have narrated in a preceding work.* I there placed before my readers the great events of that memorable epoch, and exhibited on the stormy stage of the world this Christian, whose death, even more than his life, agitated his country and all Germany. My object, in the present work, is to complete the first,—to finish the portrait of the illustrious reformer of Bohemia, by making him also known in his domestic life—the effusions of his private intercourse.

* *The Reformers before the Reformation. Fifteenth Century. John Huss and the Council of Constance.* 2 vols.

The man is completely revealed in his correspondence; and I here publish all that the friends of
Huss have handed down to us.

These Letters, which are translated now for
the first time into our tongue, were never intended for the public eye, having been addressed
by Huss to his disciples and friends, to be perused far from the view of his enemies, and
under the shade of the domestic roof. They
furnish most precious documents to history, and
are unquestionable testimonies of the spirit and
character of their author. Though they are not
remarkable either for profundity of thought, or
for style and singularity of doctrine, there, nevertheless, exhales an innocent candour and an angelic piety, like a fragrant perfume, from every
page. What especially pervades them, are the
Christian thoughts on the fall of man, and his
regeneration through Jesus Christ;—the conviction that all the things of this world pass away,
and are but the shadows of things eternal;—that
man is nothing without God;—that there is

nothing but darkness or false lights wherever the divine flame does not penetrate ;—and, lastly, above all these thoughts, subsists that which embraces all the rest—that "FAITH IS LIFE." We behold in his correspondence, a soul superior to seduction as well as to terror ; a firm and upright reason which penetrates every subtilty ;* originates in the conscience alone ; clings tenaciously to what appears to it to be the truth as to man's most precious possession, as to the treasure which has nothing to fear, neither from rust nor robber. (Matt. vi. 20.)

Huss was one of those spirits, more contemplative than practical, which, after having recognised an idea as true, admit of no medium or arrangement in propagating it, and concern themselves for the consequences not more for others than for themselves. The inflexibility of his character equalled his probity of feeling ; and it may be affirmed that, in all respects, both by the heart and the intelligence, Huss was of the

* Consult, in particular, Letter xl. of the Second Series.

number of those who appear in the world as if predestined to martyrdom. Yet he sought not after it like a passionate sectarian or a blind enthusiast; he was as far from possessing that pride which complacently feeds itself on its own conceptions, as from that sullen fanaticism which causes a man voluntarily to shorten his life by useless rashness, through dint of persuading himself that death is desirable. Before entering into a contest with his superiors, John Huss hesitated, consulted, and examined. Visited with ecclesiastical censures at Prague, he knew not whether he should obey and be silent, or continue to preach the Gospel. " I burn," says he, " with an ardent zeal for the Gospel, and my soul is sad; for I know not what to resolve on."* At a later period at Constance, when condemned and ready to die, he wrote, " I exhort you, in the name of the Lord, to detest every error that you may discover in my works; but keeping in mind this truth which I have ever had in view,

* First Series, Letter iii.

pray for me."* He faithfully depicts his feelings in a letter which he addressed at the same period to the priest Martin, his disciple, an admirable letter—a true model of prudence and every Christian virtue. " Attach thy soul to the reading of the Bible, and especially the New Testament. Fear not death, if thou desirest to live with Christ; for he has said himself, *Fear not those who kill the body, but who cannot destroy the soul.* If they should trouble you on account of thy adhesion to my doctrines, answer, I believe my master to have been a good Christian; and touching what he has taught and written, I have neither read nor understood all." Huss was neither a superstitious man nor a visionary; nevertheless he had visions and received warnings in his sleep; he foresaw what came to pass,† yet refused to attach faith to his dreams. He does not dare to place trust in them, and distrusts his senses rather than slight the authority of a single precept of his God; he repeats this text,

* Second Series, Letter xlviii.
† *Ibid.*, Letter xxxiii.

"Place no confidence in dreams;" and after having related them to his friends, he adds, "I write this not because I consider myself a prophet, or that I would exalt myself, but to shew I have suffered bodily and mental temptations as well as a great fear of transgressing the commandments of the Lord." Resignation was predominant in his mind;—the most absolute submission to the Divine will, as well as an ardent desire to become acquainted with it. "Pray," says he, "fervently to the Lord, that he may grant me his Spirit, and that I may dwell in truth, and be delivered from all evil. If my death should add to his glorification, pray it may arrive speedily, and that he may enable me to support my ills with constancy. But should it be better for my salvation that I return amongst you, we will implore of God to enable me to return from the Council without a spot, viz., that I may keep back nothing from the truth of the gospel of Christ, in order to be enabled to discover more surely its light, and bequeath to our brethren a good example to follow." The sacrifice which he made of his life was the more exemplary, and his martyrdom the more sublime, because he had felt beforehand all the terrors of death; it was in God that he sought for support against them. " Beseech the Lord to grant me the assistance of his Spirit, that I may confess his name even unto death. . . . . . I shall stand in need of his Divine aid, although I am confident he will not suffer me to be tried beyond my strength."*

His confidence in God did not forsake him to the last moment. "Our Saviour," says he, " raised Lazarus from the dead after the fourth day. He could also snatch me from prison and death,—I, an unfortunate man, if it were for his glory, for the advantage of the faithful, and my own good."† And yet, when in chains, and awaiting death, he is more occupied with the interests of others than his own; his soul, calm, pious, and compassionate, sympathizes with all

---

* Second Series, Letter xi.   † Ibid. Letter xviii.

around him; his jailors are exhorted and instructed by him. He thinks with tenderness of his disciples, of the faithful believers of his church, of his friends; the sight of his benefactors draws tears from his eyes, and he writes to them in these touching terms, "Generous Seigniors, my comforters and faithful defenders of the truth, you whom God has sent me as my angels, I cannot fully express how much I am grateful for so much constancy, and for all the charitable kindness you have shewn to me, a weak sinner, but servant in hope of Jesus Christ."*

His poverty being great, he regrets not being able to remunerate his friends who have assisted him with money. He bequeaths them all he possesses, which is but little; for the surplus of his debts he addresses an appeal, with a confidence altogether Christian, to all who are rich, and conjures them to pay for him those who are poor. He promises them, in exchange for the worldly

---

* Second Series, Letter xviii.

riches which they advance to him, spiritual and imperishable wealth.* Every word that falls from his lips or his pen affords signs of that virtue so well defined by the apostle; of that charity, so mild, patient, and benevolent, to which nothing is indifferent, because in everything it finds an opportunity of exercising itself usefully, and fulfilling a duty. At the approach of death, he feels his ardent zeal redoubled for the salvation of his brethren and dear disciples, and includes in the same solicitude all those who have listened to his preaching; and in his last exhortations no one is excepted. When on the point of appearing before the King of Heaven, all earthly distinctions vanish before his eyes; and the soul of the obscure workman is to him as precious as that of the monarch. His own soul presents an unalterable calm amidst the most cruel pains, and sometimes unbends to a sweet and tranquil gaiety. Though a prey to so many outrages, he utters neither threat nor murmur; he pardons

* Second Series, Letter xxv.

his enemies; he blesses and adores the hand of
God which tries him, and sees in these rigours
only marks of his love.

Shortly before his death he writes to his
friends thus :—" When we shall meet hereafter
in a happy eternity, you will know with what
clemency the Lord deigns to assist me in my
trials."*

Such does JOHN HUSS appear in the edifying
Letters of which we here present the translation ;
and it is impossible to peruse them without repeating, with Luther,—" If this man was not a
generous and intrepid martyr and confessor of
Christ, certainly it will be difficult for any man
to be saved."†

We have penetrated in every direction into
this mind so eminently Christian ; we have shewn
in all its aspects this soul so marked with candour and so powerful ; and it now remains to us
to assign to John Huss his place among the men

* Second Series, Letter xxx.
† Preface of Luther, page 12.

who have agitated the world, and to determine
the work which is personal to him, what, in fact,
he has left behind him that is durable. To succeed in such an endeavour, we must take into
account a prejudice which still prevailed at that
period. False notions had for centuries been in
circulation, and had taken root in Christendom,
relative to the authority of individual convic-
tions, judgment, and conscience. It was denied
that man, sustained by Divine grace, could find
in himself any assistance; it was believed to be
a meritorious act of Christian virtue to seek for
no direction in one's own internal feeling, and to
trample reason under foot; an opinion was adopted, not because in itself it had been found conformable to the Scriptures or to truth, but because it was considered to agree with the decisions of some great doctor, pope, or council, or
because it was found in Augustin, Origen, or
Jerome. Tradition alone was listened to; and
it was altogether forgotten that the first Christians, who had sprung from the Jews and Gen-

tiles, were accustomed to consult their conscience before all, in face of the altars of Paganism, or of the temple still standing at Jerusalem, and that they took for their only guide this secret and inflexible monitor. A few eloquent men— a few great minds—had, it is true, consulted their individual opinions, rather than yield to clerical and traditional authority. Abelard and Berenger, in France, had given proof of boldness and independence in proclaiming their doctrines; but they grew timid when it was necessary to defend them; their voices died away, and their heads were bowed low, before the menaces of popes and councils. In Italy, Armand de Bresse had ventured openly to resist the pontifical power; but the revolution, of which he gave the signal, was a civil rather than a religious one. Numerous sects and whole populations had, in different countries, emancipated themselves from the yoke, by depending on that irresistible force which the sympathy of the masses and the association with a whole nation creates, in order to think, believe, and suffer. England, in fine, had witnessed a powerful mind,—that of Wycliffe, nourished by the Scriptures,—bring to light a body of doctrine, from which, at a later period, sprang the code of the Reformation ;* but Wycliffe escaped alive the solemn sentence of an œcumenical council ;† and many doubt whether he could have passed triumphantly through that formidable ordeal.

It was reserved for the little town of Constance to afford a spectacle which the world had not witnessed for ages. There, one man, weakened by sickness and long imprisonment, isolated from a few friends dispersed and trembling, resisted, strong in the gospel and in his conscience, all that external authority could display to intimidate and subjugate souls. He yields not before the efforts of all the spiritual and temporal powers united. John Huss, lastly, by his

* See *The Reformers before the Reformation*, Hist. Introduct., section v.

† Wycliffe died thirty-five years before the Council of Constance condemned his memory and works.

example, still more than by his doctrines, re-opened to the Christian world a path that had been long closed; and, if it is permitted to compare sacred things with profane, effected in the sphere of religion and morality what, at a later period, Columbus brought to pass in the external and physical world; he laid open a new empire, or, to speak more correctly, he discovered a domain which had been forgotten for ages—that of the Conscience in matters of faith. Inquiry was a field interdicted to all. Huss entered on it anew, in the midst of hostile clamours, and re-opened it amidst the noise of the thunder and the tempest. He fell in his attempt; but it was important to prove that the conscience of the Christian was stronger than all the powers of the earth; for that end one of those sublime sacrifices which terminate in death was requisite. John Huss, therefore, must die; and in his death consisted his victory.

It was the firmness of his character which gave him influence over the people, like most of those whose passage through the world has left the most durable impression. He was great, especially by the heart; and although he was, by the qualities of his mind, one of the most distinguished men of his age, yet his greatness was rather moral than intellectual. He established no new system, nor attached his name to any religious creed; and his glory is, in consequence, the purer. Not being the author of his doctrines, he had no personal interest in their triumph; and the love of the truth did not, in his heart, confound itself with vanity. He was not able to obtain external liberty for religious worship; but he did more; for by his faith, by his courage before a tribunal the most elevated in the opinions of men; by the vast renown of his virtues, condemnation, and martyrdom, he caused a part of Europe to understand the sacred right of that freedom of conscience which, when properly employed, constitutes the Christian equally on the throne as in chains. John Huss, in a word, greatly contributed to bring

back Christianity to its primitive character, viz.,
that of being the religion of the heart, and to
restore its real spirit—a spirit of life, of progress, and of liberty. If Religion be not this;
if it be the monopoly of a college of priests, or
the privilege of a sect, it becomes immediately
exclusive, intolerant, and oppressive. The history of antiquity, as well as of modern times,
teaches us that men who constitute themselves
as infallible interpreters of the Divinity, make
their gods after their own likeness. The Creator
of the world would soon be no longer in their
mouths a compassionate Father, who gives to
all his children on earth an equal right of approaching him in adoration and prayer, and who
presents his word to all minds, like his Son, to
the regards of every creature; but a jealous
master, ever ready to punish and strike at the
will of his interpreters, at the cry of those who
call themselves the representatives of his power.
Religion would no longer be that celestial and
internal bond which attracts the soul to God by

love ; it would become the yoke which masters externally by constraint—a dreadful instrument of punishment to the souls which it abases, by placing them under restraint, and more destructive, if possible, to men's minds than to their bodies. It is on this account that the generous Christians of all Churches who have heroically resisted the oppressors of the conscience, are justly entitled to the imperishable admiration and gratitude of all who adore in spirit and in truth. Among these no man was ever more remarkable than JOHN HUSS ; for no other ever did more to restore to the Conscience, in the heart of man, that throne which it ought never to have abdicated.

PRELIMINARY NOTICE.

THE Letters of JOHN HUSS were collected by his friend, Peter Maldoniewitz, the notary, and it was the great Reformer of the sixteenth century, Martin Luther, who first published them, rendering justice to the faith, doctrines, and noble character of their author.   Luther at first translated into Latin four letters, written by Huss in Bohemia, and published them in 1536, together with those which the nobles of Bohemia and Moravia had addressed to the Council of Constance.   Wittemberg was the place where he published them, on the occasion of a general council being convoked by Paul III.*   He joined to these letters a preface, of which the following is an extract:—" My object in publishing these letters," said Luther, " is, if God should permit the council to assemble, to warn such persons as might be present to beware of following the example of the Council of Constance, in which the truth was exposed to such lengthened and such vio-

* This council, which was first convoked at Mantua for the year 1537, then at Vicenza, did not open until 1542, in the city of Trent.

A

lent attacks; nevertheless, it triumphs now, and, holding
erect its victorious head, shews forth that guilty assembly
in its true colours.   Undoubtedly, God has sufficiently
manifested in that council how he resists the proud, and
confounds the haughty, by their own imaginations, without paying any consideration to outward dignity."*

The following year, Luther published a complete edition of the letters of John Huss, and prefixed to it a preface which we subjoin, and in which he enumerates, with
great power, the principal claims of Huss to the esteem
and admiration of posterity.   This preface also contains
some interesting and curious details; and Luther even
narrates in it the strong impression produced on himself
in his youth, at first reading, by chance, some of the writings of that Christian whom he had been taught to exe-
crate as a dreadful heretic.   Luther is supposed to have
drawn up the summary of contents which are found at
the head of most of the letters of John Huss, in the collection of his works,† and we have most carefully preserved them.

The letters of John Huss are divided into two series,
each of which refers to a different period of his life: the

* The several editions of this Preface, which will be found at the
end of the volume (Note A), present numerous variations.   We have
considered it best to follow the first edition, which was most kindly
communicated to us by M. Frederic Monod, one of the clergymen of
the Reformed Church at Paris.

† *Hist. et Monum. Johan. Hus*, vol. i.   Nuremberg, 1715.

first is that of his interdiction and exile from Prague in the years 1410 and 1411 ; the second comprehends the period which elapsed from his departure from the council till his death.

PREFACE OF DR MARTIN LUTHER, TO THE LETTERS OF JOHN HUSS, PUBLISHED BY HIM IN THE YEAR 1537.

In order to render more prudent, and to instruct, by means of the tyrannical judgments of the Council of Constance, all theologians that may be hereafter called to sit in a council of the Roman Church.

Should any man read these letters, or hear them read, being, at the same time, in possession of a sound intelligence, and, in the face of God, having a regard for his own conscience, he will not, I am convinced, hesitate to allow that John Huss was endowed with the precious gifts of the Holy Spirit. Observe, in fact, how firmly he clung, in his writings and his words, to the doctrines of Christ; with what courage he struggled against the agonies of death; with what patience and humility he suffered every indignity; and with what greatness of soul he at last confronted a cruel death in defence of the truth;—doing all these things alone and unaided, before an imposing assembly of the most powerful and eminent men, like a lamb in the midst of wolves and lions. If such a man is to be regarded as a heretic, no person under the sun can be looked on as a true Christian. By what fruits, then, shall we recognise the truth, if it is not manifest by those with which John Huss was so richly adorned?

The greatest crime of John Huss was his having declared that a man of impious life was not the head of the universal Church: he allowed him to be the chief of a particular church, but not of the universal one; just the same as a minister of the word, whose life is criminal, still remains minister according to external appearance, although he is not, on that account, a member of the saints in his church. In a similar manner, John Huss denied that an impious and flagitious pontiff was a worthy one, although seated on the throne of the Church; it is as if we should declare that Judas, being both traitor and robber, was not an honest man, although he had been called to the functions of an apostle. Every effort, in fact, was made to prevail on John Huss to admit that a criminal pope ought to be regarded as a saint, and was infallible; that his words and acts were alike holy, and ought to be received and respected as so many articles of faith. All the men of the Council of Constance, wise as they were considered, would have lent a favourable ear to such assertions,—they who, when they had dethroned three culpable pontiffs, did not allow to any one the right of condemning them to the flames! But when John Huss said the same things, they dragged him at once to the stake!

The door was (once more)* thrown open to similar events, by the indulgences which the Roman pontiff scattered with such profusion over the whole world, and by the jubilee which he instituted at Rome to build the church of St Peter: for the pope, amongst his other inventions, declared, and afterwards confirmed by his bulls, that the souls of such persons as, having undertaken a pilgrimage to Rome, should happen to die on the way, should at once take flight to heaven; and, in his quality of God on earth, and God's viceroy, he orders, most peremptorily, the angels to bear such souls upwards on rapid cars. Tetzel, the bearer of the indulgences of the bishop of Mentz, in like manner taught that the souls would spring from purgatory to heaven, as soon as the clink of the money paid into the treasury should be heard; but when shortly after he was confounded and put to shame, he shut his impudent mouth.

It was to oppose such impieties, calculated as they were to disgust even a brute animal,† that John Huss, preacher of the Word of God at the chapel of Bethlehem at Prague, put himself forward. He denied that any such power was given to the Roman pontiff, who, he boldly declared, might

* We add these words, omitted by Luther, but necessary to complete the meaning of the passage.

† " Quos nullus neque asinus neque porcus ferret."

be mistaken in that as well as many other things. Having then taken the great liberty of inculcating that the pope can err (a heresy then considered far more frightful than to deny Jesus Christ), he was constrained by violence to confirm what he had maintained in saying, that an *impious pope* was not a *pious* one. All then were in wild commotion, like so many wild boars, and they gnashed their teeth, knit their brows, bristled up their coat, and, at last, rushing precipitately on him, delivered him cruelly and wickedly to the flames.

One of the first articles that it was necessary to admit at that period was, that the Roman pontiff was infallible; and such was the opinion of the jurisconsults of the Roman court. It did not appear presumable that any error could emanate from so elevated a quarter; but when personal presumptions are formed, it often comes to pass too much is presumed.

The extraordinary mistake of these men on so important a point, and the manifest outrages which John Huss suffered from them, only served to animate him with greater courage. A conscience pure of all crime before God and before the world, affords a man a great consolation in his misfortunes; and if his suffering should be for the name and glory of God, the Holy Spirit, the Comforter of the afflicted, immediately comes to his aid, and lends him assistance against the world and against demons, as Christ has promised (Matt. x.) in these words:

" It is not you who speak, but the Spirit of your Father who speaks in you ;" and (Luke xxi.) " For I will give you a mouth and wisdom, which all your adversaries shall not be able to resist and gainsay."

I have heard from some persons worthy of faith, that the Emperor Maximilian said, in speaking of John Huss, " They have done great injustice to that excellent man." Erasmus of Rotterdam, in his early writings, now in my possession, has declared that John Huss had been burned, but not convinced; and the general opinion amongst pious men of that day was, that he had been loaded with outrage and violence. I will relate here what Dr Staupitz narrated to me of a conversation which he had with his predecessor, Andrew Prolès, a man of birth and merit, relative to the rose of Dr John Zacharias. This Zacharias was represented in the cloisters bearing a rose in his hat, as a distinction for him, and an affront to John Huss. Prolès, seeing this image, said, " I would not consent to wear that rose." Staupitz having inquired for what motive, Prolès replied, " When it was maintained before the Council of Constance against John Huss, that the pope could not be represented by any one, Dr Zacharias brought forward the passage of Ezekiel (chap. xxxiv.), *It is I who am above the shepherds, and not the people.** John

---

* It is not easy to see, in reading this recital, what force the adversaries of Huss could draw from the passage, for the Eternal is alone spoken of, who announces that he comes himself in the place of bad

Huss denied that these words could be found to form part of the chapter alluded to ; and Zacharias offered to prove the contrary, from the very Bible which John Huss had brought from Bohemia : for Zacharias, like many others, had often visited Huss for the purpose of convincing him, and he had by chance happened to perceive the passage in question. The Bible was then produced in the assembly, and it shewed that Zacharias was right. John Huss, nevertheless, maintained that the Bible was not a correct one, and that the other versions would not confirm it ; but being overwhelmed by the clamours of his adversaries, he lost his cause, and Zacharias received a rose from the Council, in perpetual memory of this fact. And yet," observed Prolès, " it is certain that these words are not found in any correct Bible, whether manuscript or printed, and that they all testify against Zacharias." Such was the account of Prolès to Dr Staupitz.

The verse alluded to is found in all German, Latin, Greek, and Hebrew Bibles, as it was quoted by John Huss ; but at Constance they could not admit it in any other way than as quoted by Zacharias, who deserved neither to receive the rose nor to wear it.

The adversaries of John Huss's opinions have them-

pastors. The argument of Zacharias cannot have any weight except with those who absolutely behold God in the pope, and who imagine that all that is said of the Eternal in the Scriptures is applicable to the pope.

selves testified to his learning. Thirty years back, I heard several able theologians declare that " John Huss was an exceedingly superior doctor, and that he surpassed in erudition and knowledge all the persons composing the council." His writings, and, amongst others, his *Treatise on the Church*, and his *Sermons*, confirm this eulogium.

When I was a divinity student at Erfurt, my hand happened to alight, one day, in the library of the monastery, on a volume of John Huss's sermons. Having read, on the cover of the work, the words, *Sermons of John Huss*, I was immediately inflamed with a desire to ascertain, by perusing this book, that had escaped from the flames, and was thus preserved in a public library, what heresies he had disseminated. I was struck with amazement as I read on, and was filled with an astonishment difficult to describe, as I sought out for what reason so great a man—a doctor, so worthy of veneration, and so powerful in expounding the Scriptures—had been burned to death. But the name of Huss was, at that period, such an object of execration, that I absolutely believed that if I spoke of him in terms of praise, the heavens would fall on me, and the sun veil his light. Having then closed the book, I withdrew sad at heart, and I remarked to myself, by way of consolation—" Perhaps he wrote those things before he fell into heresy."

At that time I was still ignorant of what had passed in
the Council of Constance.

All that I could say would only add infinitely to the
high character of John Huss. His adversaries render
him a striking, though unintentional testimony; for if
their clouded eyes could open to the light, they would
blush at the remembrance of the things which they themselves narrate. The author of a collection of the acts of
the council, written in German, and enriched with very
many remarkable details, endeavours, with all his power,
to cover with odium the cause of John Huss; and yet
he declares, that when Huss beheld himself stripped of
all the dignities of his order, he smiled with intrepid
firmness. According to the same author, also, Huss,
when conducted to the funeral pile, constantly repeated—
" Jesus, Son of God, have pity on me!" At the sight of
the fatal stake to which he was to be fixed in order to be
burned, he fell on his knees and cried out—" Jesus, Son
of the living God, who suffered for us all, have pity on
me!" Beholding a peasant bringing some wood to feed
the flames, he again smiled with mildness, and uttered
these words of St Jerome—" O holy simplicity!" * A
priest having drawn nigh, and demanded if he desired to

* Luther here confounds two events. The touching expression which
he mentions is erroneously attributed to John Huss; it fell from the
lips of Jerome of Prague.—(*Vide " The Reformers before the Reformation."*
Vol. II., Book III., Chap. XII.

confess, Huss replied, that he was ready to do so; and the priest having insisted on the necessity of abjuring, John Huss refused, saying that he did not consider himself guilty of any mortal sin.

The man who, in the agony of death, invoked, with so firm a heart, Jesus the Son of God—who, for such a cause, delivered up his body to the flames with so strong a faith, and so stedfast a constancy—if such a man, I repeat, deserves not to be considered a generous and intrepid martyr, and true follower of Christ, it will be difficult for any one to be saved. Jesus Christ himself has declared:—" He who confesses me before men, him will I also confess before my Father." What more shall I say? The Roman pontiff raises many men to the rank of saints, of whom it would be difficult to predicate if they are with the elect or with the devils; and he precipitates into hell a man like this, when it results, from the examination of his whole life, that his place is in heaven. *

I have again specified these matters, in order that they may serve as a salutary warning to such of our theologians as may repair to the approaching council; for should they resemble the men who assembled at the Council of Constance, the same thing will happen to them as to their predecessors—the acts which they will

---

* Luther adds :—" Sunt igitur in numero sanctorum tuorum diaboli, et tu vicissim in ipsorum, mi pontifex Romane."

be anxious to conceal and bury in oblivion shall be
dragged forth to the open day, aud published everywhere.   The doctors of Constance were convinced that
no person would ever presume to accuse them, either by
word or writing, and much less in the teeth of the cruel-
est menaces, to honour John Huss as a saint, and condemn them for their conduct.   Events have, on the
contrary, either by me or by others, verified the predictions of John Huss.   Our theologians, strong in their
authority, anticipate no peril.   I admit their power to
be equal to what they possessed in John Huss's time ;
but it is not less certain, that he who then stood at their
tribunal now sits in a place where his judges must give
way before him.

LETTERS OF JOHN HUSS.

ATTESTATION OF PETER MALDONIEWITZ, CALLED THE NOTARY.

These pages are all faithfully copied from the Letters of John Huss, written with his own hand, and they correspond, word for word, with the originals.*

FIRST SERIES.

LETTERS WRITTEN AT THE PERIOD OF THE INTERDICTION OF JOHN HUSS, AND OF HIS EXILE FROM PRAGUE IN 1411;—SOME OF THEM MAY HAVE BEEN WRITTEN IN 1410.

The letters of this series contain the greater part of the admirable exhortations addressed by John Huss to

---

* This attestation of the faithful Maldoniewitz is found after John Huss's letters, in the old collection of his works.—*Johann. Hus. Hist. et Monum.* vol. i., p. 95.

the believers of his church.   They are not distinguished either for the great diversity of incidents, or the dramatic interest of those in the second series, but they clearly evidence the great intrepidity, Christian piety, love for his brethren, and true greatness, that pervaded the mind of Huss.   The writer already felt a presentiment of his martyrdom ; and it is easy to perceive in reading them, that he would not give way when his time was come.*

LETTER I.

TO THE COLLEGE OF CARDINALS.†

[In this letter, John Huss complains of having been falsely denounced, and humbly demands to be dispensed from being obliged to appear in person.   For the same purpose, John Huss makes an appeal to John XXIII.,‡ which has been in-

* For historical details relative to this period of the life of John Huss, see *The Reformers before the Reformation*, vol. i., book i.

† Of all the letters that have been saved of John Huss, this is the only one addressed to his ecclesiastical superiors, the dignitaries of the Church.   It is valuable, inasmuch that it shews the respect with which he addressed them, his ardent desire to convince them of the purity of his doctrines, and the fear which he felt of a rupture, without any mixture of weakness.

‡ It is in the text, *Scripsit ejus totam;* but this pretended letter is the act of appeal drawn up at Prague before a notary, June 23. 1410. —(*Hist. et Monum. Johan. Hus.* vol. i., p. 112–116.)

serted in his history, accompanied by the testimony of the
Academy of Prague.]

I write with the humble submission and respect that
is due to your commands, Reverend Fathers in Christ;
you who are clothed with an apostolical character, who
shine as great lights to enlighten the nation, and who
are elevated to power in order to efface the sins of the
world, to snatch souls from the snares of Satan, and to
succour those who suffer in Christ's name.* I would
humbly have recourse to your fatherly counsels, incapable
as I am of supporting the burden which weighs me down.
The evils that overwhelm me date from the time that a
portion of the Church withdrew their obedience from
Gregory XII. I then recommended with success, in my
sermons before the Barons, Princes, Clergy, and People,
their adhesion to the College of Cardinals, for the union
of my holy mother Church. It comes to pass that the
Reverend Father in Christ, Sbynko, Archbishop of
Prague, an adversary of the Sacred College, caused a
pastoral letter to be affixed to the doors of the churches,
prohibiting all the masters of the University of Prague,
and in particular myself, from exercising any functions
of the sacred ministry, under the pretext that the masters of the University of Prague, who had adhered to the

---

* John Huss attached to the acts of good priests the efficacy which
the Roman Church attributes indefinitely to those of all priests.—
See *The Reformers before the Reformation*, vol. i., book i.

Sacred College, had withdrawn their allegiance from our Holy Father Gregory XII. and the Holy See.   But facts must be judged by their results, and it occurred that the Archbishop was constrained, by the decrees of the Council of Pisa, to approve of the conduct of the masters.— Such was the first origin of the accusation laid against me, and of all my troubles.

The Sacred College of Cardinals having promised many favours to their adherents, I have kept in remembrance these promises, and have placed trust in them, as one should do in the promises of those who are the pillars of the Church.   I therefore implore your Reverences, and on my knees I conjure you, to cast a regard of kindness on my misfortune, that I may be dispensed from appearing in person,* and from other most painful obligations resulting from it.   I am innocent of the things of which my adversaries accuse me; and of this I call to witness our Lord Jesus Christ.   I am willing to appear in the presence of the University of Prague, of all the prelates, and of all the people who came to hear me, and before them to give, by word and by writing, a full and absolute account of the faith that I guard in my heart, and to confess it, even at the peril of being burned to death.† Your Reverences may be assured of this confession by public documents as well as by the testimony of the University of Prague.

---

* Before the pope.   † " Etiam igne ad audientiam porito."

LETTER II.

TO ZAWYSSIUS, HIS CALUMNIATOR.

Grace to you and peace from our Lord Jesus Christ. It has come to my ears that you have accused me of heresy. If this be true, send me word, and you shall know then, by the grace of God, what is the faith which I confess, which I defend, which I do not dissemble in the shade, but which I profess as becomes a true Christian. And, would to God that your eyes might be opened as to the manner in which, for nearly thirty years, you have shorn your flock in Praschatitz. Where do you dwell? How do you labour? How do you feed your flock? You have forgotten these words of the Lord:— " Wo unto the shepherds, who only care for themselves, and do not feed their sheep!" Tell me, I pray you, are you penetrated with that part of the gospel of Christ, which says—" *The good shepherd goeth before his sheep, and his sheep follow him; for they know his voice.*" The time will come when you must render an account of your sheep and of your numerous benefices, concerning which it is said in your own ordinances, that he who can live upon one, cannot retain another without committing a mortal sin.

Meditate, then, on these things, and accuse not your neighbour of heresy. If you know him to be a heretic, you ought to warn him, according to the Apostle's precept, a first and a second time; if he refuse to listen to you, avoid him; and even should you be chosen to condemn him, still you must demonstrate by the Scriptures, that you condemn him justly, and deliver over his books to the flames.

I write you these few lines, to warn you fraternally, according to the precept of Christ, which tells us:—" If thy brother has just sinned, warn him in secret." Receive, then, my words, my brother, and declare, if you have thus spoken of me. Prove that I am a heretic, and I will, with humility, correct myself, and you shall receive a reward for having rescued a man from error. Nevertheless, I hope by the grace of Almighty God, that my faith in our Lord Jesus Christ is as great as yours, and that I am not less prepared to die for it with humility.

LETTER III.

TO MASTER MARTIN AND TO MASTER NICOLAS OF MYLIEZYN.

[He consults them on the subject of the interdiction pronounced against him from the pulpit.*]

May peace be with you, that peace that is not given with the world, with the flesh, and the devil. The Lord has said :—" You shall have tribulations in the world ; but if you persevere in well doing, who can do you harm ?" I burn with an ardent zeal for the gospel ; and my soul is sad, for I know not what to resolve on. I have meditated on these evangelic words of our Saviour (John, chap. x.) :—" The good shepherd giveth his life for the sheep. But he that is an hireling and not the shepherd, whose own the sheep are not, seeth the wolf coming, and leaveth the sheep and fleeth : and the wolf catcheth them and scattereth the sheep."

I have also meditated on these words from St Matthew, (chap. x.) :—" But when they persecute you in one city, flee ye into another." Of these two precepts, so different to each other, which ought I to follow ? I know not.

* He also asks his friends whether he ought to quit his church ; and it is probable that he wrote this letter before leaving Prague.

I have meditated on the letter of St Augustin, to an illustrious bishop, who consulted him in a like case. Augustin thus terminates his answer :—" He who takes to flight, and does not deprive, in so doing, his church of the evangelical ministry, does what the Lord has commanded him; but he who, in his flight, takes away spiritual food from the flock of Jesus Christ, is an hireling, who, when he sees the wolf approaching, fleeth, because he careth not for his sheep. It is because thou hast consulted me, well-beloved brother, that I write thee these things, which appear to me to be according to both truth and charity; but I invite thee not to follow my counsel, if thou findest a better. What can be more advisable, in such an extremity, than to offer up prayers to God to have pity on us, after the example of some holy men, who have obtained by their prayer, not to abandon the Church of God, and who have persevered in their good resolutions, even in the very teeth of their enemies?" Such is the opinion of St Augustin.

Inform me, then, if you acquiesce in these words; for although the necessary aliment of God's Word is not wanting to my flock, my conscience reproaches me with my absence, as a scandalous act.

I fear, on the other hand, that my presence during the term of my interdiction might be the means of tearing this food away from my flock, and of depriving them of the Holy Communion and other advantages, which concern Salvation.   Therefore, let us pray humbly to Almighty God, that he may deign to reveal to us what I ought to do in the present circumstance, in order that I may dwell in the right way.   The advice that the blessed St Augustin expresses in his letter, is wise : he establishes in fact, that in circumstances where we may be anxious for ourselves alone, flight is permitted, and he cites on the point the example of St Athanasius ; but should the whole flock be exposed, we must resign ourselves to our lot, in order to do what may prove most useful to the Church.

LETTER IV.

TO THE RECTOR OF THE UNIVERSITY OF PRAGUE.

Venerable Rector, I have received great consolation from your letter, in which you declare, amongst other things, that "the just man shall not be afflicted, whatever may befall him ;" from which you infer, that temporal tribulations, and my separation from my friends, ought not to discourage me, neither sadden nor cast me down, but, on the contrary, should fortify and make me glad.   I accept with gratitude this consolation.   I cling to the

words of Scripture, and say, If I am just, no trouble, whatever it may be, could sadden me, so as to turn me from
the path of truth. If I live, and wish to live holy, in Chris
it is necessary that I suffer persecution in the name of
Christ; for as it was necessary that Christ should suffer in
order to enter into glory, we also should bear our crosses,
miserable beings as we are, and should imitate him in his
passion.

I protest, then, venerable Rector, that I have never
felt myself overwhelmed by persecution; that I am only
borne down by my sins, and by the errors of the Christian
people. What, indeed, are the riches of the world to me?
What affliction can their loss cause me? What is it to
me to lose the favour of the world, which makes us swerve
from the path of Christ? What signifies infamy, which
when supported with humility, proves, purifies, and illu
minates the children of God in such a manner, that they
shine and radiate, like the bright sun, in their Father's
kingdom? And, lastly, what is death, if this miserable
life be torn from me? He who loses it in this world triumphs even over death, and finds true life in the next.

But men, blinded by luxury, vainglory, and ambition,
understand not these things. Others are turned away
from the truth by fear, and languish on in a strange per-
plexity, deprived of charity, patience, and of every other
virtue. On the one hand, they are urged on by knowledge
of the truth; and, on the other, by the fear of losing their

reputation, or of exposing their wretched bodies to death. For my own part, I will expose mine to it (I trust with the assistance of our Lord Jesus Christ), if his mercy comes to my assistance; for I do not desire to live in this corrupted age, unless I can lead to repentance myself and others, according to the will of God. This is what I ardently desire for you; and I exhort you, as well as all those united to you, to hold yourselves ready for the combat; for behold already appear the preludes to the beginnings of Antichrist: the combat is near, and the poor bird* must flap his wings against the wings of Behemoth, and against this tail of Antichrist, that always engenders abominations.

The prophet has shewn it to us when he declares, that he who teaches falsehood is the tail of Antichrist, and a grave old man is the head. The Lord will confound both one and the other; he will confound the pope and his preachers, his officers and his doctors, who, under a false name of holiness, conceive abominations. What greater abomination is there than that of the prostitute, who abandons herself publicly to every comer? Nevertheless, the abomination is greater still of him who, sitting in high places, offers himself, as if he were God, to the adoration of all;† traffics in spiritual things, and sells all

---

* John Huss alludes to his name, which, in the Bohemian, signifies goose.

† " Adhuc major est abominatio bestiæ, quæ parata est a quocumque veniente adorari."

that he possesses not. Woe, then, unto me if I preach not against such an abomination! Woe unto me if I weep not, if I write not against it! Can you find one man for whom such things are not a calamity? Already the great eagle takès its flight and cries to us: " Woe! woe to the inhabitants of the earth!"

LETTER V.

TO JOHN BARBAT.

[Huss consoles him, and justifies himself by exposing why he preferred obeying God, who had commanded him to preach, to the pope, the archbishop, and all those who had prohibited him from so doing.]

I salute you in the name of our Lord Jesus Christ!

I have learned, my beloved friends,* your grievous affliction. Look upon it as for your good; for it is to bring to light your firmness and your constancy, that you have fallen into various temptations.

I also, my very dear friends, have been tempted; and

* Although this letter was more particularly addressed to John Barbat, Huss intended it to be read to several others.

I rejoice at last that I am called a heretic for the gospel's sake, and excommunicated like a rebellious and wicked man. To fortify in me the sweet calm of my soul, I have called to mind the life and words of Christ and the Apostles (Acts, iv.). I remembered in what manner Annas, the high priest, and Caiaphas, and John, and Alexander, and all the kindred of the high priest, when they addressed the Apostles, prohibited them from speaking and teaching in the name of Jesus. *" But Peter and John answered and said unto them, Whether it be right in the sight of God, to hearken unto you more than unto God, judge ye. For we cannot but speak the things which we have seen and heard."* And when the same priests prohibited them a second time from preaching, they replied (Acts, v.), *" We ought to obey God rather than man."*

It is true that the pagans, the Jews, and the heretics, all regulate their conduct on this precept of the obedience that is due unto God. Alas! this maxim blinds those who are not Christians, but not the Apostles, nor the true disciples of Christ.

St Jerome says :—" If the master or bishop prescribes what is not contrary to the faith or the Scriptures, the servant should obey. But if he commands what is contrary to these, we must rather obey the Master of the soul, than the master of the body." And in another place he adds :—" If the emperor orders you, to

B

do that which is good, execute the will of the emperor; should he require you to do ill, answer, ' It is better to obey God than men.' "

St Augustin also says, in his *Sermon on the Words of the Lord :*—" If my earthly presence commands that which you ought not to do, despise this power, and fear a higher one.   Consider the different degrees of human power.   Do you obey the under officer, if the proconsul orders you the contrary?   And if the proconsul orders you to do one thing, and the emperor another, would you attempt to disobey the latter for the former?   If the emperor commands you to do that which is prohibited by God, despise the emperor and obey God.   We ought, then, to resist the power of the devil or of men, when they suggest any thing against God ; and in doing so, we resist not, but obey even God's commands."   Such are the sentiments of St Augustin.

Gregory also says, in his last *Treatise on Morality :*— " Know, therefore, that evil should never be done from mere obedience."   St Bernard writes in one of his letters :—" To do evil after the orders of any one, is not to obey, but to disobey."   And St Isidore maintains, that if he who is in authority does and orders a thing which is not according to the Lord, or violates the written law, and orders it to be overstepped, to him ought to be applied these words of St Paul : " If an angel should descend from heaven, and preach to you a gospel different from that which we preach, let him be accursed!" He also declares, that whoever forbids you to do what is commanded by the Lord, ought to be held in execration by all who love the Lord—he ought to be regarded as a false witness and a sacrilegious person.

It would appear from these words, that these names are applicable to those who interdict the preaching of the Divine Word, and that such persons are excommunicated according to the words of the Prophet, " Cursed be those who resist thy commandments !" Jerome expresses the same feeling as is experienced by myself, when he thus writes to Rusticus, Bishop of Narbonne :— " Let no bishop abandon himself to envy and anger, through an infernal jealousy, because the priests exhort the people, preach in the churches, and bless the multitude." I declare, then, to those who prohibit me to do these things, that he who interdicts priests from doing that which God commands, professes himself to be superior to Jesus Christ.

Bede, in speaking of our Saviour, repeats this passage :—" Go ye into the village that is over against you, and immediately you shall find an ass tied, and a colt with him : loose them, and bring them to me : and if any man say any thing to you, say ye, The Lord hath need of them; and straightway he will let them go." Jesus Christ, says Bede, teaches mystically the doctors, by these words, that if they meet with any obstacle, if any one prevents them from freeing sinners from the bonds of the devil, from drawing them to God in confessing the faith, they ought not, for this reason, to renounce preaching his word, but should, on the contrary, continue to insinuate it into their souls; for the Lord has need of such labourers to edify his Church. Who could, in fact, quote all that the saints have written, when teaching us, that it is better to obey God than man?

Our oppressors oppose to us these words:—" All, therefore, whatsoever they bid you observe, that observe and do," (Matth. xxiii.); but they are reduced to silence by the prohibition which follows :—" But do not ye after their works." God says, (Deut. xxiv.)—" Do according to all that the priests the Levites shall teach you : as I commanded them, so ye shall observe to do." The Lord desires, therefore, that he who obeys, should only do so after his own commandments. It is also said, (1 Pet. ii.)—" Servants be subject to your masters with all fear." And the Apostle further adds :—" Not only to the good and gentle, but also to the froward." Not, however, in things in which they are wickedly inclined ; for that would be to obey the devil. The will of God and the Holy Scriptures, therefore, teach us, that obedience to superiors is obligatory only in lawful matters. I have clung firmly to this truth, and have preferred in my sermons, to inculcate obedience to God, rather than to the pope and the archbishop, or any others that may oppose this saying of Christ.

I put my name to these words, in order to teach you how to confront the emissaries of the devil.*

LETTER VI.

TO THE BELIEVERS IN PRAGUE.

[He felicitates them on the constancy with which they listen to the word of God.]

John Huss, a servant of Jesus Christ in hope, to all those who love God, who confess his law, in expectation of the Saviour, with whom they desire to live for all eternity!

Grace be with you, and the peace of the Lord Jesus Christ, who offered himself as a victim for our sins, to deliver us from this world of affliction, and from eternal damnation, according to the will of God the Father, to whom be glory for ever and ever!

Dearly beloved,—Having learned your zeal and your

* " Ut sciatis canibus diaboli obviare."

progress in the word of God, I render thanks unto the Lord, that he has deigned to enlighten you to such a point that, perceiving the frauds of antichrist and his ministers, you may not allow yourselves to be turned away from the truth.

I feel a lively confidence that his mercy will crown the work of regeneration commenced in you, and that he will not permit you to turn aside from the truth, whence many diverge through fear of danger, apprehending man, a weak sinner as he is, more than the all-powerful God, who has power both to kill and bring to life; to destroy and to save; to preserve his faithful believers in the midst of grave and numerous perils; and to give them in exchange for a brief space of suffering an eternal life of inexpressible happiness. Wherefore, beloved, do not let yourselves be borne down by terror; and do not be frightened if the Lord should tempt some of you, by allowing the ministers of antichrist to exercise their tyranny over you. God himself has said to his servant, (Prov. iii.), " Be not afraid of sudden fear, nor of the power of the wicked falling upon thee; for the Lord will be at thy side, and will keep thy foot, that thou be not taken." And he has also said, by the mouth of his prophet David, " I am with him in his day of trial : I will deliver him."

Knowing that, dearly beloved, consider, with St James, that it is fortunate for you to fall into various temptations; because the trial of your faith worketh in you patience, and that contributes to render you perfect and entire, failing in nothing.

St James also says,—" Blessed is the man that endureth temptation ; for when he hath been proved, he shall receive the crown of life, which God hath promised to them that love him." Remain steadfast, therefore, in the truth, and act in every thing like true children of God. Have full confidence ; for Christ has overcome, and you will overcome also. Remember always Him who suffered so much at the hands of sinners ; relax not in your good resolution ; but, laying down together the whole burden of your sins, rush to the combat with your eyes fixed steadfastly on Jesus, who established our faith, and who, for a glorious object, despising shame, suffered the ignominy of the cross, and is now seated on the right hand of God.

The Creator, the King, the Sovereign Master of the world, without being forced to it by his Divine nature. humbled himself, notwithstanding his perfection, to our nature. He came to the assistance of us, wretched sinners, and supported hunger, and thirst, and cold, and heat, and fatigue, and want of sleep ; he suffered, whilst instructing us, sorrow, and grave affronts from the priests and scribes, to such a point that they called him a blasphemer, and declared him to be possessed of a devil, averring that **he was not God, whom they excommunicated as a heretic,** whom they drove out of their city, and crucified like one accursed.

If, then, Christ supported such things from the priests —he who healed all kinds of diseases, without any earthly recompense, by his word alone; who cast out devils, raised the dead, and taught the word of God; who never did injury to any one; who committed no sin, and who endured every thing from his enemies, because he discovered their wickedness;—if he supported such things, why should we be astonished that the ministers of antichrist, who are more avaricious, more debauched, more cruel, and more cunning than the Pharisees, now persecute the servants of God, overwhelm them with insult, excommunicate, imprison, and kill them?

Remember what our Lord and our King said:—" If the world hate you, know that it hated me before you. If you were of the world, the world would love you as being of it; but because you are not of the world, and because I have chosen you out of the world, the world hates you. Remember what I say unto you; the servant is not greater than his master: if they have persecuted me, they will persecute you also; they will do all these things to you on account of my name, because they have not known Him who sent me."

Remember also the prophecy of our Divine Saviour, which declares that his elect will suffer persecution from the world, that is, from the wicked, who know neither God the Father, nor our Lord Jesus; for although they confess with their lips that they know God, yet they deny him by their reprobate actions. It is of them that St Paul spoke to Titus, when he declared that their works are avarice, simony, debauchery, and contempt of the word of God, placing human traditions above the word of God, and performing no work of humility, charity, temperance, and Christian love.

Therefore is it, that the wicked will not cease to persecute the saints as long as the war lasts between Christ and antichrist; for St Paul has told us, that all who desire to live purely in Christ shall suffer persecution, but the wicked shall advance in the path of perdition, always deceived, and deceiving others.

St Paul teaches us by these words, that all pious men will suffer persecution for Christ's sake; the wicked will be seduced, and will seduce others, and their heart will swell with malice for their own destruction. It is of them that our Saviour has spoken in these words:—" Behold, I send you forth as sheep in the midst of wolves; be ye therefore wise as serpents, and harmless as doves. But beware of men; for they will deliver you up to the councils, and they will scourge you in their synagogues. And ye shall be brought before governors and kings for my sake, for a testimony against them and the Gentiles. They shall scourge you; the brother shall deliver up the brother to death, and the father the child ; and the children shall rise up against their parents, and cause them to be put to death ; and ye shall be hated of all men for my name's sake, but he that endureth to the end shall be saved." This persecution shall last till the day of judgment.

The Lord spoke in this way to his disciples, in order that they might, if possible, escape from such evils. He elevated their understanding, that they might be prudent, and might be able to recognise, by their works, the devouring wolves whose voracity would swallow up the whole world.

He also shewed them by what signs they might know false prophets, the latter not agreeing with the true prophets, either in the explanation of the Holy Scriptures, or in their works. There are false Christs, calling themselves the chief disciples of Christ, and yet who prove themselves, by their works, to be his greatest adversaries. These will seek, by every means, to smother and suppress the Word of God ; for it condemns their insolence, pride, avarice, simony, and other evil works.

They have made an irruption into the churches and places of worship, to prevent the Word of God being preached there ; but Jesus Christ has not permitted them to bring their criminal undertaking to a prosperous end. I understand that they intend destroying the chapel of Bethlehem, and that they interdict sermons in the other places where the Word of God is taught. But

I feel a firm confidence that God will not permit them to succeed. They wanted to entwine the simple bird * in the snare of citations and anathemas; and they have already set their ambush even for some of you. But if that bird, which is a mere domestic fowl, whose flight is circumscribed, and far from lofty, has broken through their nets, how much more will other birds, that soar aloft as they announce the Word of God, despise such ineffectual wiles. They have thrown their nets, and displayed their anathemas, like the image of a bird of prey, to cast terror all around; they have flung about their fiery darts from the quiver of antichrist, in order to prohibit the Word of God and His worship; but the more they strove to disguise their real nature, the more they rendered it visible; and in seeking to stretch forth their traditions like nets, they broke them to pieces; in their anxiety to gain the peace of the world, they destroyed not only it, but, at the same time, the spiritual peace; and in their attempts to injure others, they wounded themselves most.

What happened to the priests of the Jews has befallen them; for they have lost that which they were endeavouring to retain, and have fallen into what they were striving to avoid. They hoped to succeed in stifling and putting down the truth, which always conquers; and they

* Huss alludes here to his own name, which, in Bohemia, signifies " *goose.*"

were ignorant that its very essence and characteristic consisted in this, that the more attempts were made to dim its lustre, the more it shone brightly forth—the greater the endeavour to suppress it, the more it soared aloft.

Pontiffs and priests, the scribes and Pharisees, Herod and Pilate, and the inhabitants of Jerusalem, formerly condemned the Truth; they crucified it and buried it; but it rose from the tomb and conquered them all, sending forth in its stead twelve preachers of the Word.

This same Truth, instead of acting feebly and inefficiently, has sent to Prague mighty eagles, surpassing all other birds, by their piercing sight, and which, by the grace of God, fly aloft in the air, and win over others to Jesus Christ, who will strengthen all those who are faithful to Him. He has said—" I will be always with you, even unto the end of the world." If, then, God, the most powerful and just of defenders, is with us, what evil work can prevail against us? What fear, what death, can separate us from Him? In what shall we be the worse, if, for His sake, we were to lose our friends, the honours of the world, or even our miserable life itself? We shall, at last, be delivered from our load of misery; we shall receive a hundredfold riches infinitely more precious, friends more dear, delight more perfect, of which death cannot despoil us; for he who dies for Christ will surely partake the triumph: he is freed from all

TO THE BELIEVERS IN PRAGUE.

misery of every kind, and enjoys eternal bliss, to which our Lord Jesus Christ deigns to conduct us all !

Beloved brethren, and sisters no less dear to me, I write you this letter, that you may remain fervent in the truth, which you have acknowledged, and that you may not pay less attention than before to the Word of God, on account of the cruel threats of his enemies ; for God is faithful to you, and will both strengthen you and keep you from evil.

In fine, I beseech you, dearly beloved, to pray for those who, with the grace of God, announce the truth ; pray for me also, that I may write and preach still more against the malice of hell, and that God may accord me in this combat that support which is so necessary in order properly to defend his Word. You know that I do not hesitate to expose this miserable body to the peril of death for God's truth, being well aware that nothing will be wanting to us in his Word, and that his Gospel must be propagated more and more every day. Moreover, I desire to live for those who suffer violence, and who have need of the preaching of the Word, in order that the malice of antichrist may be laid open, and the good not be made its victims. I preach, there-fore, in other places, and I officiate for those of whom I speak, being convinced that God's will must be accom-plished in me, whether I suffer or die by antichrist. But should I proceed to Prague, I am certain that snares

will be there laid for me, and that you will be persecuted
by my adversaries, who serve not God, but prevent others
from serving him.   We pray to God for them, however,
that, if any of the elect should happen to be amongst
them, they may be converted to the truth.   May God
accord you full understanding of these things which I
write you ; may he grant you perseverance ; and may
your heart be worthy of all these blessings, through the
merits of Jesus Christ, who suffered for us the most cruel
and ignominious death, leaving us his example, that we
may suffer the same, according to his holy will.   Amen.

LETTER VII.

TO THE SAME.

[The same subject.]

The grace and peace of our Lord Jesus Christ be with
all the believers in Prague who sincerely love his holy
Gospel !

I, John Huss, the servant of God, do supplicate and
conjure you, well-beloved, not to abandon the truth which
God, in his mercy, has imparted to you.   That power

which has begun to operate in us, whom he has chosen
out, will continue, I feel convinced, still to do so, and
will give us, in our temptations, perseverance and
strength. I myself only live by his mercy and grace.
I can declare, with St Paul, " For me to live is
Christ, and to die is gain. But if I live in the flesh,
this is the fruit of my labour: yet what I shall choose I
wot not. For I am in a strait betwixt two, having a
desire to depart and to be with Christ; which is far better : nevertheless, to abide in the flesh is more needful
for you. And having this confidence, I know I shall
abide and continue with you all, for your furtherance and
joy of faith." So did St Paul write from his prison in
Rome to the Philippians.

I also say unto you, dearly beloved, that although I
am not in prison, I would willingly die for Christ, and be
with him; and I say also that I should be well pleased to
preach to you again the Word of God, for your salvation.
I do not know which of these would be for the best ; for
I have full confidence for myself in the mercy of God,
and also fear that some evil may arise amongst you,
which may occasion persecutions against the true believers, and be the cause of eternal perdition to those
who believe not. These rejoice and desire most ardently
not only to smother in me the Word of God, but also to
shut the asylum of Bethlehem, where I have preached
the Gospel of Christ to you; but if God consent not,

their efforts will be vain; and if he permit it, such a misfortune will come to pass on account of the wicked, as Bethlehem, where the Lord was born, and Jerusalem, where he redeemed us, were seen to be overwhelmed to the lowest foundation.

As to us, let us render thanks to God, submitting constantly to his divine power, which always assists those who love Him, and sets those free who suffer for His sake, allotting their persecutors to eternal torments. I beseech you, therefore, brethren, not to let yourselves be cast down, but rather to pray to our Saviour Jesus Christ to give you constancy to persevere in the faith to the end; and be persuaded that he will accord you the free and unmolested preaching of his Word, and that he will augment your strength in order to defend you from the fury of that antichrist, against which he has prophesied in his holy Scriptures.

LETTER VIII.

TO THE CHURCH OF PRAGUE.

Master John Huss, servant of God, to all who in Prague are the elect of God, and who love our Lord Jesus Christ and his Word, wishes mercy and peace from God the Father, and our Lord Jesus Christ.

Dearly beloved, I congratulate you on your listening assiduously to the Word of God; and our merciful Saviour will assuredly send you firm and faithful guides. May God, through our Saviour and Lord Jesus Christ, grant you mercy, peace, and grace, for all good things, in order that what you have well commenced in him, you may conclude in like manner, and may persevere in doing so even unto the end. Acknowledge, therefore, and draw on you the mercy of God, who sent his Son into this world for our sakes; who allowed his Son to become man, and to be humiliated, despised, and condemned by all, to such a point that, when the people were called in by the priests to choose between two prisoners, they delivered, in preference to Jesus Christ our Saviour, a robber and murderer, and laughed to scorn our Lord, who said, by the mouth of Jeremiah, " Lend an ear, and behold my anguish ;" and again, " See if any pain is comparable to mine."

He cried out to his Father, " My God, Why hast thou
forsaken mē ?"   Such were his plaintive words whilst suffering on the cross an ignominious death, and exposed to
the blasphemies of the priests, who insulted him at the
foot of the cross, exclaiming, " He put his confidence in
God; let God deliver him if he can!   Thou who couldest
destroy the temple, now come down from thy cross!"   His
cry was, " My God, Why hast thou forsaken me ?"   And
why did he utter that exclamation ?   In order that we
may recognise and admire his immense mercy; and that,
supporting with him the outrages of the wicked, we may
look for our refuge in Him alone : in order, in fine, that
we may publicly shew our gratitude for his Divine compassion, which has redeemed us from everlasting damnation.

Such has been towards us the mercy of our Lord Jesus
Christ, who recommended his disciples to say, into whatever house they entered, " Peace be with you!"   And
when he raised up the dead, he said to them also, "Peace
be with you!"   And before his death, when conversing
with his disciples, " I leave you my peace!"   Wherefore,
dearly beloved, I implore him to accord you that same
peace.   May peace be with you from the Lord, that you
may live honestly and soberly—in calm, in justice, and
in piety; and that you may conquer your enemies and
those of God—the devil, the world, and the flesh.   Peace
be with you from the Lord, that you may love each other,

and your enemies also. Peace be with you, that you may listen to his Word with attention and humility. Peace be with you, that you may speak wisely and well, and that you may escape from your enemies. Peace be with you, that you may learn how to be silent with advantage ; for whoever listens with humility never disputes evil-mindedly with any one; he who speaks prudently triumphs over the fool ; and he who is silent in proper season, rarely acts against his conscience.

On account of all these things, may peace, grace, and mercy be with you! peace, that you may have a tranquil conscience; grace, that your sins may be forgiven you; and mercy, that you may be delivered from unquenchable fire! May, then, peace be with you all, after this miserable life, in the bosom of eternal felicity, from God, the Father, and our Lord Jesus Christ. Amen.

LETTER IX.

TO THE HEARERS OF THE WORD OF GOD AT PRAGUE.

[He fortifies them, and inspirits himself against the anathemas of the pope.]

I, Master John Huss, &c. &c., call on you, dearly beloved, not to allow yourselves to be disturbed on account of my absence, or on account of the maledictions with which the enemies of God overwhelm me. I have faith in my Saviour, and I feel confident that all things will happen, both to you and to me, for our good. Only beware of sin, and pity the fate of those who, believing that they are acting well, oppose God and his holy Word : like the Jews of old, who crucified Jesus Christ and stoned Stephen, and of whom both Christ and Stephen said, " They know not what they do." They cannot hurt me, whether they prepare my cross with blasphemy; or overwhelm me, like another Judas, with abuse which they shout out in public ; or, in fine, fling stones against the gate of the temple, and overthrow it. In doing such things, it is against themselves that they labour; and it is they who ought to tremble.

They have imagined certain practices of worship in conformity with human ordinances, in order to subject to their will men of simple minds, and induce such to follow them ; but God will bestow on his believers the knowledge necessary to discern such practices, and to recognise in them mere human traditions, by means of which their inventions lead astray weak minds, separating them from the law of God, and crushing them to the earth, by terrifying them with the thunders of anathemas.

God enjoins to pray for such men as we believe to be in error, and to declare them condemned of God ; but he has not ordered such snares to be laid in his temple against innocent men. Perhaps, to judge by their letters, they act in memory of the eternal damnation of Dathan and Abiram, who, unworthy as they were, had presumed to pretend to the priesthood.

They designate, by these letters, all the priests who improperly usurp the sacerdotal functions through love of riches, pleasure, dignities, or other gratifications of the flesh. They pour out anathemas, and vociferate like senseless disciples of Judas, as simonists and reprobates really are. Let us pray to God, dearly beloved, that he may deign to continue to us his blessings : no anathema will then be able to reach us, but the Sovereign Pontiff, Jesus Christ, will bless us, saying, " Come ye, blessed of my father, receive the kingdom which was prepared for you from the beginning of the world."

Let us eagerly long for this blessing, dearly beloved; let us seek for it and await its coming, living piously in this world, in order to enjoy eternal life in the regions of heaven, by the merits of Jesus Christ our Lord, blessed for ever and ever.

LETTER X.

[Huss, whilst reminding believers of all the benefits with which
  the Lord has loaded us in his first coming, elevates their souls
  to the expectation and hope of the second coming and final
  judgment.]

John Huss, servant of God, to all believers, peace
and mercy from God the Father of our Lord Jesus
Christ.   Strengthen your hearts, dearly beloved, for the
coming of our Lord Jesus Christ is nigh.   You know
that Christ has come once already; ponder on it therefore, and fortify your hearts by grace, and by the trial
of affliction.   Reflect, dearly beloved, that the Son of
God, himself God Eternal, became man, and humbled
himself in order to help us.   The immortal Physician came
to heal our incurable sores : the all-powerful Lord came,
not to trouble the dead, but to vivify the living, and redeem his elect from eternal death.

The King of the world, the Supreme Pontiff, came to
accomplish, by his works, the law of God.   He came into
the world, not to rule over the world, but to give his life
for the redemption of a great number.   He came, not like
a usurer, to swallow up the riches of the world, but to
redeem, by his blood, those whom sin had sold to the devil.
He came, omnipotent as he is, to suffer a bloody and ig-

nominious death from the Pharisees under Pontius Pilate, in order to free us from the power of Satan. He came not to destroy the elect, but to save them; as he himself has said, " I have come that they may have life ;" that they may have life here by his grace, and still more abundantly in eternity; that everlasting life, reserved for all the elect, which is unattainable to the proud, the luxurious, the avaricious, the violent, the ambitious, the intemperate, the effeminate—all, in fact, who are opposed to his words; but which shall be enjoyed by the elect alone, who listen to his law, who accomplish it by their works, and who suffer persecution.

Meditate, therefore, in your souls on these benefits which our Lord Jesus Christ has heaped on us by his first coming, and strengthen your hearts, dearly beloved, by grace and affliction; for the second coming of Jesus Christ is near, and, with it, the sentence of the Great Judge, infinitely wise, infinitely just, infinitely formidable, from whom neither the great nor the learned of this world can escape; whom they can neither move by favour nor by gifts; and with whom will come the just, the preachers of his Word, and all that have been unjustly persecuted in the world.

Nigh, then, draws the judgment of that severe and redoubtable Judge, whose regard the wicked will not venture to encounter; the judgment of Him at whose word all iniquity will be laid open : at his command the bodies of the evil-doers shall be delivered to the flames, and their souls shall dwell for all eternity with the devils, after having heard from the mouth of God that just and terrible sentence, "Depart to the everlasting fire prepared for the devil and his angels."

Meditate, then, dearly beloved, on these two things—the benefits of the Saviour at his first coming, and his justice and judgment at his second advent—and fortify your hearts by grace and the cross. And when you suffer, arouse yourselves; lift up your heads (that is to say, your minds), for your deliverance is nigh at hand,—your deliverance from every misery, and from the eternal damnation which we shall be saved from at the voice of that equitable Judge, who has said, "Come to me, blessed of my Father, receive the heavenly kingdom that is prepared for you." Amen.

LETTER XI.

TO THE SAME.

[John Huss justifies himself, by the example of Christ, for having quitted Bethlehem.]

Dearly beloved, the birth-day of the Son of God is near at hand; purify, therefore, your dwelling, and let it be clean of all sin; listen attentively and piously, according to your opportunity, to the Word of God, and pay no attention to the evil-doers who forbid you to meet at Bethlehem. They have endeavoured to lead you astray on account of me, and now they no longer have that motive. As for those who declare that I took to flight, I can reply, that I acted of my own free will, in order to obey the Divine Word, and follow the example of him who has said— " And whosoever shall not receive you, nor hear your words, when ye depart out of that house or city, shake off the dust of your feet as a testimony against it. And if you are persecuted in one city, flee to another." And when the Jews sought to put him to death before his hour was come, he often withdrew himself from their hands. St John, in fact, has written—" Jesus therefore walked no more openly among the Jews; but went thence unto a country near to the wilderness, unto a city called Ephraim, and there continued with his disciples." But the Jews sought for him, and often asked amongst themselves— " Why comes he not on a feast day?" For the priests and Pharisees had ordered whoever should discover his retreat, to inform them of it, in order that he might be followed. It is not, therefore, surprising that, in compliance with such an example, I should have withdrawn, and that the priests should ask where I am.

Learn then, dearly-beloved, that it is through the example and recommendation of Christ that I removed to a

c

distance from you, through fear of being to the wicked an occasion of eternal condemnation, and to the good a cause of sadness and mourning. I fled, in order that impious priests might not prohibit the preaching of the word of God, and that you might not be deprived, on my account, of the Divine truth, for which, by the grace of God, I am ready to die. Know also, dearly beloved, that it was necessary that Christ should suffer within the period prescribed by his Father. Be assured, that whatever God may have determined in relation to me, his will shall be done; and should he deem me worthy to die for his name, he will summon me to martyrdom; but if, on the contrary, my life is to be prolonged for the preaching of his word, in like manner that is also in his will.

Undoubtedly, some of your priests desire my return to Prague, and would willingly see me there again, in order to their chanting the offices and the mass being dispensed with: it is they whom the holy preaching of the Gospel offends, on account of their avarice, their pride, and their adulteries. But you, who love God's word, and who make every effort to unite yourselves to him, would be well pleased to see me, and would gladly have me amongst you in a spirit of charity, like one of your dear friends. For my part, I long to behold you again, in order to be able to announce to you God's word; for the principal care of the ministers of the Church ought to be to announce, in all sincerity and with fruit, the gospel of Christ, in order that the people may be acquainted with the will of God, may avoid many evils, and be led into the right path for living irreproachably. Woe, then, to such priests as neglect the word of God! Woe to them who, when they can announce it, live nevertheless in effeminacy and idleness! Woe to them who prevent the word of God from being preached and listened to!

Happy, on the other hand, are they who attend to it, who guard it in their hearts, and who preserve it in themselves by good works. Christ has blessed them, saying, —" Happy are they who hear the word of God, and keep it." May Christ, blessed for evermore, augment for us all this great happiness! Amen.

LETTER XII.

TO THE SAME.

[He celebrates the joys and blessings of our Lord's birth-day.]

My very dear brethren, Although I am separated from you in body, not being perhaps worthy to preach to you any longer the word of God, nevertheless, the love with which I yearn towards you constrains me to approach and address you in a few words. This is the day, dearly be-

loved, on which the angel of the Lord said to the shepherds—" Behold, I bring you good tidings of great joy,
which shall be to all people." And immediately, a multitude of the heavenly host were heard to cry out,—
" Glory to God in the highest, and on earth peace, good-
will toward men."

Knowing that, dearly-beloved, rejoice; for, this day a
Child is born of inestimable price, a man-God, in order
that glory may be to God in the highest, and on earth
peace, good-will toward men. Rejoice; for, this day is
born for us a Mediator, that man may be reconciled with
God, and that this peace may be spread over the earth.
Rejoice; for, to us is born a Physician, to make sinners
pure from sin, to deliver them from the power of Satan,
to redeem them from eternal damnation, to impart to all
a heavenly joy, that glory may be to God on high, and on
earth peace, good-will toward men. Rejoice; for, to us is
born a King, to fill us with joy; a High Priest, to pour on
believers the Divine blessing; a Father, to adopt us as his
children for all eternity. To us is born a well-beloved
Brother, a Master in every kind of knowledge, a veritable
Chief, a Judge of most perfect equity, that glory may be
to God on high, and on earth peace, good-will toward
men. Rejoice, sinners, for He who is born is the Son of
God, the High Priest who absolves all that repent, in
order that glory may be to God on high, and on earth
peace, good-will toward men. Rejoice, for this day the

holy bread, that is to say, God has made himself food for men, in order to satisfy, with His body, all that hunger. Rejoice; for, this day is born the Redeemer of the world, the Saviour of sinners. Rejoice; for, this day an immortal God is born, in order that mortal man may live for ever. Rejoice, for the Lord of the universe lay poor in a stable, in order that our poverty might be changed into riches. Rejoice, dearly-beloved, that the predictions of the prophets and of the saints have been fulfilled. Rejoice, for the omnipotent Father and the Son, abounding in wisdom and grace, are given to us, that glory may be to God on high, and on earth peace, good-will toward men. Rejoice, then, dearly-beloved, for the angel said—" Behold, I bring you good tidings of great joy." And what was that joy? That a Saviour was born who would deliver us from all our miseries, and free us from sin. The Son of God is given us, that great joy may be with us, and glory to God on high, and on earth peace, good-will toward men. Let us endeavour to insure that this Infant which is born to us may accord us that good-will, that peace, and that joy, which lasts for ever and ever. Amen.

LETTER XIII.

[He impresses on the believers of Prague the necessity of zeal, and
of a desire to hear God's Word, and recommends them not to
renounce these things on account of the scandals arising from
wicked preachers.]

I desire ardently, dearly-beloved, that you may be delivered by Jesus Christ from all your sins, and that, despising the vanities of this world, you may overcome the
world, the flesh, and the devil. I am anxious that,
through the grace of our Lord Jesus Christ, you may
suffer all things with patience, with a view to salvation,
and that you may persevere even unto the end in your
trials and afflictions. That is what I demand for you,
dearly-beloved, in my prayers ; for God is my witness
that I laboured for upwards of twelve years in the vine-
yard of the Lord, and that my greatest consolation in
my ministry was to perceive your zeal in listening to the
divine Word, and the serious repentance of a great
number.

Wherefore, dearly-beloved, I conjure you, by the passion of Jesus Christ, to hold firmly to his Gospel, and so
to conduct yourselves that it may bring forth fruit in all
your actions. Be not shaken in your faith, and regard
not those who, having placed only an uncertain foot in

the path, have turned aside elsewhere, and have become the most violent enemies of God and of his disciples.

You know, dearly-beloved, that Christ's disciples, who held converse with him, withdrew, and refused to follow him farther. Yet Christ came to separate men from one another, for he has said—" I have come to separate the son from his father, and the daughter from her mother." And also—" You shall be delivered up to men, and persecuted for my name's sake." And in order that we may not be shaken by this abandonment of his disciples, or frightened by persecution or death, our Saviour added —" A hair of your heads shall not fall without the will of God." If, then, a single hair cannot perish, how can believers themselves perish? Wherefore, dearly-beloved, preserve a real faith and a sure hope; remain steadfast in the love of God's Word; listen with the most ardent affection to those whom the Saviour has sent you, in order that they may preach his Gospel with constancy, and resist the devouring wolves and false prophets of whom Christ has spoken, when he said—" False prophets will come, and will lead astray many." Christ teaches believers to beware of them, and to recognise them by their works, which are avarice, simony, contempt of God's Word, persecution of believers, calumny, zeal for human traditions, &c. These men, in fact, wear sheep's clothing: they assume the externals of the Christian, and, as they are, within, devouring wolves, they rend and devour Christ's flock. It is of such that

Christ has said to his disciples :—" Behold, I send you as sheep in the midst of wolves ; be, then, prudent as serpents, and simple as doves." Let them be prudent, said he, that they may avoid, like serpents, to allow themselves to be crushed, and to permit the head of the Church of Christ to perish in them : let them be simple as doves, in order to suffer with patience the cruelty of the wolves. And we, dearly-beloved, already behold these wolves clearly before us ; but let us not suffer them to lead us astray, and turn from the path by which we are striving to arrive at heavenly joys.

Preserve firmly faith, hope, charity, humility, mildness, justice, modesty, temperance, sobriety, patience, and the other virtues, adorning yourselves with good morals and good works. Rejoice that you suffer persecution, for Christ has said—" Blessed are ye when men shall hate you, and shall reproach you, and cast out your name as evil, for the Son of man's sake. Rejoice ye in that day, and leap for joy ; for behold your reward is great in heaven." Who, then, is there that possesses faith, hope, and charity, who will not support with patience, contempt, and ignominy, for the love of his Saviour, when he is well assured of receiving a hundredfold advantage in everlasting life ?

In the expectation of these things, remember this saying of Christ, that " an affliction shall come such as never had been seen from the beginning of the world."

And 'why? the Apostle tells us—"that a time shall come when men will not receive the sound doctrines, but will listen to false teachers with greedy ears;" they will leave the truth and cling to fables. Thus is now accomplished the prophecy of St Paul, who declares, that all who desire to live purely in Christ will suffer persecution; and the impious will triumph in their ruin.

Receive, therefore, dearly-beloved, the exhortation of St Peter; beware of allowing yourselves to be led astray with others, by the error of the wicked; do not permit your mode of life to be disturbed; but increase in the grace of God, in the knowledge of Jesus Christ, and pray that God may graciously accord happy success to my preaching, wherever a want of it may be felt, in the towns and villages, fields and forests, in every place where I may be useful, in order that the word of God may not be stifled in my mouth; uphold and console each other under the protection of God the Father, of his well-beloved Son, and of the Holy Spirit, who can preserve you from all evil, and procure for you eternal joy. To him be praise and glory for ever and ever. Amen.

LETTER XIV.

TO THE INHABITANTS OF THE TOWN OF LUNA.

[John Huss recommends union, and teaches them to endure insults rather than to avenge them.]

Master John Huss, an unworthy servant of God, to
the believers residing in the town of Luna. Peace, and
the protection of our Lord Jesus Christ, be with you !

My very dear brethren, Although I cannot see you externally with my eyes, but only with my mental vision, I am
nevertheless acquainted with your charity and your constant faith in God and in his Gospel. I know that the
Saviour has united you in faith, peace, charity, and attention to his word, so that I find amongst you, more
than in any other town of Bohemia, that concord which
so deeply rejoices my heart. I conjure you, therefore,
dearly-beloved,—I whose features are unknown to you,
but who am attached to you sincerely in God—I conjure
you, in the interest of your salvation, to love one another ;
to remain united, and to let no man come between and
divide you ; for this precious unity, which subsists between you by the true faith, will save you in the presence
of God ; and God, through his mercy, will, in return,
give you strength to overcome the world, the flesh, and
the devil.

Meditate on these things, dearly-beloved, and allow no schisms, or treachery, or jealousy, or violence, to spring up amongst you. Should any obstinate disseminator of disturbance and discord arise amongst you, warn him like a brother, but do not enter into any disputes before the judges or courts of law; for that would cause the destruction alike of your fortune, body, and soul. Study to avenge the insults offered to God, rather than your own. Alas! it is in this point that the whole world is mistaken; for all men are more ready to avenge their own injuries than those of God. And that is the broad path opened by Antichrist; and, above all, dangerous to us who are priests, and who desire to see the ordinances of men more rigorously observed than the commandments of God. Such, or such a priest, monk, or prelate, is a fornicator or adulterer with impunity, and yet he insists on having his own ordinances observed, under pain of excommunication! In like manner, they do not inflict punishment on the laity who sin against God; but should one of them presume to say—" My brethren, you have unjustly condemned me!" they at once strike with the sword, because any one has raised his voice against the injustice of his clerical judge.

I have full confidence that the Lord will keep you free from these evils, so that you may observe his word rather than the ordinances of men. As long as you observe his word, no one can do you harm. Wherefore, dearly-beloved, meditate deeply on these two things, which are eternal and imperishable—condemnation and ever-lasting life. The former will draw you into fire that lasts for ever, dreadful torments, and a devouring and endless sojourn with devils; but in eternal life all will be perfect joy, absence of affliction and suffering, and a residence with God himself and his angels. For, as St Paul says—" Eye hath not seen, nor ear heard, neither hath entered into the heart of man, the things which God hath prepared for them that love him." We shall, therefore, be indeed blessed when we enjoy this beatitude, of which the delights will be perfect and without drawback, and we shall then behold who shall be condemned;—there all sins hidden in the hearts of men shall be laid bare; there we shall reap a joy and a consolation of which we shall never be deprived; there, in fine, we shall be happy if we suffer anything here for Jesus Christ; for, as gold is tried by fire, so shall we be proved by the cross and by affliction, under the hand of Him that has produced the world from nothingness. We shall therefore be happy, if we persevere to the end in well-doing.

Let us bear in mind, dearly-beloved, that the world is wasting away, that death is at hand, and that we are here only on a pilgrimage. Live, therefore, first of all piously, renouncing your sins; next, aspire to heavenly joys; and, lastly, love God with all your heart, and have confidence in him, that he may deck you out with his glory, through the merits of Jesus Christ, and may make you sharers in his reign.   Amen.

LETTER XV.

THE PRIEST WYCHEWITZE TO JOHN HUSS AND HIS FRIENDS.

To you, dearly-beloved in the Lord, be salvation and all that is most precious in the bosom of Jesus Christ— to you whom I love in the truth, and not I alone, but all who have knowledge of the truth that dwells in you, and will always remain there, through the grace of God ! I felt a most lively joy when our brethren came and bore testimony to your true doctrine, informing us of the manner in which you walk in the light.   I have learned, dear brethren, with what rigour Antichrist is proving you, by inflicting on believers various and most grievous tribulations ; and I feel no astonishment, if, amongst you, as already almost everywhere in the world, the law of Christ has such violent assaults to sustain from his enemies.   Let us, then, strengthen ourselves in the Lord our God, and in his infinite goodness : and let us be confident that he will not permit his faithful followers to wander aside from their object, provided we love him as we ought to do, with all our heart. There would be no suffering borne by you, if iniquity did not abound. Be not, therefore, shaken by any tribulation, or any trial, supported for the sake of Christ ; for we know with certitude, that they whom the Lord judges worthy to be his children, are proved by him in affliction : our merciful Father sends us persecutions in this miserable world, in order to receive us afterwards into his grace. The great Workman proves and purifies the gold, before he receives it into his incorruptible treasury : the period of our life here below is brief and transitory : the life which we hope for hereafter is full of delight, and eternal. Let us, therefore, labour whilst we can to secure our being admitted into this happy rest. What do we behold in this perishable life, if not grief and mourning, and what ought above all to afflict the faithful,—a too great abandonment and contempt of the law of God.

Let us, then, strive to attain, as much as is necessary, to durable and eternal things, detaching our souls from those which pass away and perish. Consider the ancient fathers, the saints of the old and new alliance : have they not all traversed this same ocean of tribulation and persecution ? Were not some sawed in two, others stoned, others put to death with the sword ? All have passed by a difficult road, and so followed the footsteps of Christ, who said, " Let him who serves me, follow my steps." Wherefore, placing before you the example of so many saints who have preceded us, and being pressed on all sides by sin, let us patiently await the combat which is offered us, our eyes fixed on the foundation of our faith—on that Jesus who suffered the trial of the cross; let us implore him who suffered every indignity from the hands of sinners to support our souls; let us combat firmly against his enemies, loving his law, and not being false workmen; but let us act faithfully, and labour for the Lord, in the hope of an eternal reward.

Thou, my dear Huss, my well-beloved brother in Christ, although my eyes have never beheld thee, thy features are well known to me by faith and affection; for this world cannot disjoin those whom the love of Christ strongly binds together. Rejoice in the grace that has been accorded thee: exert thyself like a valiant soldier of Christ: preach and exhort, by thy word and thy example: recall all that thou canst into the way of truth; for the truth of the gospel ought not to be held back on account of some vain censures and antichristian excommunications. Impart, then, strength to the members of Christ that are enfeebled by Satan; and even should Antichrist be raised to the very topmost point of power, his reign will soon finish. I rejoice, above all, that in your kingdom, and elsewhere, God animates hearts, that support with joy, captivity, exile, and even death, for Christ's word.

What more shall I say to you, dearly-beloved? I know not; but I confess that my heart would dissolve with delight, if I could thus strengthen and console myself under the law of the Lord. I salute, from the bottom of my soul, all the believers and faithful disciples of the truth; and, in particular, Jacobel, thy coadjutor in the preaching of the Gospel, requesting him to pray in his church to the Lord for me.

May the God of peace, who raised from the dead the Shepherd of the sheep, Jesus Christ, our Sovereign Lord, render you capable of all well-doing, in order that by his acting with you as he may deem fit, you execute his will. All your friends, who have heard your constancy spoken of, salute you. I desire most ardently to receive a letter from you; for be assured that it affords me no trifling consolation.

Written at London, on the day of the Nativity of the Virgin, in the year of our Lord 1410.*

---

* The signature runs thus :—" Vester servus cupiens in labore fieri socius, Ricus Wychewitze, infimus Sacerdotum."—This letter has been erroneously attributed by several historians to Wyckliff.

SECOND SERIES.

LETTERS WRITTEN BY JOHN HUSS, AND OTHER PER-
SONS, AT THE PERIOD OF THE COUNCIL OF CON-
STANCE.

The letters of this Second Series were all written in the
nine months which elapsed between the departure of John
Huss for the Council, in October 1414, and the last day
of June 1415, which immediately preceded his execution.
They form one of the most curious monuments of this
celebrated period, and present an irrefragable testimony
in favour of John Huss against his judges. We perceive
in the early ones, by the eagerness of the populations to
flock to him on his passage, how great was already the
authority of his name and doctrines in Germany. In
reading those which come after, we are present at the
grand scenes of the Council; and had we not the con-
cluding ones before us, we should never perhaps know to
what a degree this man, so intrepid and so firm in his
faith before God and men, was to the end filled with gratitude towards his benefactors, torn with solicitude for

his flock, full of love toward his friends, and actuated by feelings of mercy towards his persecutors.

The letters of this series were collected without order of date by Peter Maldoniewitz, and were so published by Luther. We have classified them with great care, some from the indications given by Huss himself, and the rest in the order of the events which they narrate. Some letters of Huss's friends have been included in the collection, and add to the interest of this correspondence, at once so dramatic and so truly Christian.*

---

* For the history of this period of Huss's life, consult *The Reformers before the Reformation*, vol. ii., book iii.

LETTER I.

TO MASTER MARTIN.

[John Huss wrote this letter previous to his departure from Bohemia, and left it sealed up in the hands of the person to whom it was addressed, requesting it not to be opened until after his death.]

Master Martin, my much beloved brother in Christ, I exhort thee to fear God, to keep his commandments, and to watch over thyself when in female company. Be provident in listening to their confessions, that Satan may not deceive thee by honied words; for Saint Augustin has said—"Trust not thyself to devotion; for corruption is sometimes the greater in proportion as the devotion is apparent; and disordered passions may conceal themselves under a mask of piety. . . Beware, then, of incurring an irreparable loss: and I trust you will remain pure from all commerce with women, for I have taught thee, from thy youth upwards, to serve Jesus Christ.* Know, therefore, it is for having condemned the avarice

* Ergo cave ne irrecuperabilem perdas, quam spero retines, virginitatem; memento quia a juventate tua docui te servere Christo-Jesu.

and disorderly life of priests, that, by the grace of God, I suffer a persecution, which will soon be extinguished by my death. I do not fear to be confounded for the name of Jesus Christ.

I conjure thee not to seek after benefices. Nevertheless, if thou art called to a cure, let the glory of God, the salvation of souls, and labour alone, occupy you, and not the possession of riches. If thou shouldst obtain a church, take not a young woman for servant, and avoid ornamenting thy house more than thy soul; above all, bestow thy cares on the spiritual edifice; be pious and humble with the poor, and consume not thy estate with feasting. If thou dost not amend thy life, and abstain from sumptuous clothing and superfluities, I fear that thou mayest be chastened, as I myself am,—I who have used such things, seduced by the custom and approbation of the wicked, and troubled by a spirit of pride which is in opposition to God. From thy youth, thou hast known my preaching and private exhortations; it is, therefore, useless to write thee more; but I conjure thee, by the mercy of our Lord, not to follow me in any of the vanities into which thou hast seen me fall. Know, alas! that before receiving the priesthood, I lost much time in playing at chess, and through this game often suffered myself to be provoked, as well as provoked others to anger. I recommend myself to thy prayers before God, for this sin, and for my other innumerable transgressions. I invoke his mercy for me, that he may deign to direct my life, and that after the victory over the perverse powers of this age, over the flesh, the world, and Satan, he may open to me at the day of judgment the celestial country. Adieu, then, in Jesus Christ, with all those who keep his laws. Receive my grey gown as a mark of my remembrance of thee ; nevertheless, if thou art ashamed of the grey colour, dispose of it for the best, and as thou thinkest proper. Thou wilt give my white gown to the Curé, my disciple ; thou wilt also give to George or to Suzikoñ, sixty silver groschen, or my grey gown, because he has faithfully served me.

Outside the letter, Huss wrote—

I conjure thee not to open this letter before thou hast ascertained the certainty of my death.

LETTER II.

JOHN HUSS TO THE BOHEMIANS PREVIOUSLY TO HIS SETTING OUT FOR THE COUNCIL.*

I, John Huss, in hope, priest and minister of Jesus Christ, to all our well-beloved and faithful brethren and

* This letter was written in Bohemia by Huss; several translations of it were made by his adversaries to injure him before the Council.

sisters, who have heard from my mouth the divine word, and who have received the mercy and peace of God and of the Holy Ghost, I pray they may continue to walk without blame in the truth as it is in Jesus Christ.

You know, dear brethren, that for a long time I have instructed you in the faith, teaching you the word of the Lord, and not things foreign to the truth; for I have always sought, seek now, and shall seek unto the end, your salvation. I had intended, before I set out for Constance, to refute the false testimonies, and confound the false witnesses, who wish to bring me to the scaffold, but time has not permitted me, and I will do it at a later period. You, then, who know these things, think not, suppose not, that I encounter unworthy treatment for any false doctrines. Dwell in the truth, and confide yourselves to the mercy of God, who has given you the truth through me, his faithful preacher, to know and defend the truth, and beware of false teachers. . . . . . . As to me, I am setting out to travel with a safe-conduct from the Emperor, to meet and confound my numerous and mortal enemies, as will appear clearer than the day, when they stand before me and produce against me their false testimonies.

Mine enemies in the Council, more numerous than were Christ's, are found amongst the bishops, and doctors, and also amongst the princes of this age, and the Pharisees. But I confide myself entirely to Almighty God my Saviour ; I hope, therefore, he will grant my ardent prayer, and put prudence and wisdom in my mouth, that I may be able to resist them ; that he may bestow on me his Holy Spirit to fortify me in the truth ; so that the gates of hell shall not be able to lead me from it, and that I may face, with an intrepid heart, temptation, imprisonment, and the sufferings of a cruel death.

Christ has suffered for his well-beloved ; should we, then, be astonished at his leaving us his example, in order that we may patiently suffer all things for our own salvation ? He is God, and we are his creatures ; he is the Lord, and we are his servants ; he is the Master of the world, and we are but frail mortals ; he is not in want of anything, and we are utterly destitute ; he has suffered, and should not we suffer also, especially when suffering is unto us a purification ? Truly, he who confides in Christ, and dwells in his truth, cannot perish. Therefore, my beloved brethren, pray to him incessantly to bestow his Spirit upon me, that I may dwell in the truth, and be delivered from all evil ; and if my death should contribute to his glory, pray that it may come quickly, and that he may give me strength to support my afflictions with constancy. But if it be better, in the interest of my salvation, that I should return amongst you, we will ask of God, that I leave the Council without a blemish ; that is to say, that I may keep back nothing of the truth of the gospel of Christ, in order that we may distinguish its light more purely, and leave to our brethren a fine example. Probably you may never again see my countenance at Prague; but if the will of Almighty God should deign to restore me to you, let us advance, then, with a better heart in the knowledge and love of his law. The Lord is merciful and just, and gives peace to his children in this world and after death. Let him watch over you who has purified us by the sprinkling of his precious blood—of that blood which is the eternal pledge of our salvation! May he permit you to accomplish his will; and when you shall have accomplished it, may he bestow on you peace and eternal glory, through Jesus Christ, with all those who have dwelt in the truth!

LETTER III.

LETTER WRITTEN FROM NUREMBERG TO HIS CONGREGATION AT PRAGUE.

Salvation be to you through Jesus Christ! Learn that from the day I left Bohemia, I have travelled on horseback, and without concealment, my face being uncovered. As I approached Pernau, I found the Curé and his vicars waiting my arrival. When I entered the town* he drank

---

* Huss adds, *in stubam;* but the sense which he attached to this word is doubtful.

a large cup of wine to my health, and, with his vicars, listened, in a spirit of charity, to my doctrine, and said that he had always been my friend. All the Germans saw me afterwards with pleasure in the new town. We went from thence to Weyden, where we beheld a great crowd, as if in admiration; and when we had come to Saltzbach, I said to the consuls and ancients of the city: " I am that John Huss, of whom, without doubt, you have heard so much ill spoken. Behold me; assure yourselves of the truth, by interrogating me yourselves." After much questioning, they received perfectly well all I said to them. We *afterwards* traversed Inspruck, and passed the night in the town of Lauff, where the Curé, a celebrated jurist, came, accompanied by his vicars. I had a long conference with him; and he also received my words with great attention. We arrived next at Nuremberg, where some traders, who preceded us, had announced my arrival; which caused the people to assemble in the thoroughfares, demanding which was John Huss. The Curé, John Heluvel, wrote to me before dinner, stating his wish to have a long conversation with me. I invited him to come, and he did so. The citizens and masters afterwards assembled together, in the desire of seeing and conferring with me. As soon as they came, I rose from the table and went to meet them; and as the masters desired to argue with me, I told them that I spoke in public, and that all who wished to listen should hear me;

and from that moment until night-time, we discussed religious matters in the presence of the consuls and citizens.

There was present a doctor whose words were deceitful; and I perceived that Albert, Curé of Saint Sebold, saw, with pain, the approbation given to my doctrines. Nevertheless, all the citizens and masters remained satisfied. "Master," said they, "truly, all that we have just heard is catholic; we have ourselves taught these things for many years; we have held them to be true, and still consider them such; truly you will return from this Council with honour." We separated in the best terms with each other. Know that I have not yet met with an enemy; and in all the hotels where I stop I am well received. No hatred is stronger against me than that of some men from Bohemia. What more can I say to you? The nobles, Wenceslaus, and John de Chlum, act piously and nobly towards me. They are like heralds and advocates of the truth. God assisting, all goes on well. The Emperor is in the kingdom; Wenceslaus Lesma follows him, and we shall arrive in the night at Constance, where Pope John is shortly expected. We understand he follows the Emperor at a distance of sixty miles.

[Written at Nuremberg on the Sunday before the festival of the Eleven thousand Virgins.]

LETTER IV.

JOHN, CURÉ OF JANOWITZ, TO THE FAITHFUL BELIEVERS OF PRAGUE.

[Fragments of a letter attributed to John, Curé of Janowitz, and inserted in the latin collection of John Huss's letters.*]

Very dear Friends, I desire you to be informed that an auditor of the Sacred Apostolical Palace came to our lodging with the Bishop and the Ecclesiastical Judge of Constance. They conversed with the master ;† and there has been a long debate between the Pope and the Cardinals on the subject of his interdiction. They have decided a messenger should go from them to the master, and inform him that the Pope, of his full power, suspends the interdiction and sentence excommunicating him, and prays him, in order to prevent scandal and public rumour, not to present himself in places where the Pope and the Cardinals solemnly officiate ; granting him otherwise full liberty to visit the town, the churches, and all other places he pleases. We have understood that they all fear the next sermon which Master John intends delivering to the clergy ; and, in fact, some one yesterday—we know not whether a friend or an enemy—spread the report that

---

* This letter is important, as it shews in what manner Huss was treated during the early part of his stay at Constance.

† With John Huss.

John Huss will preach to the clergy next Sunday in the Cathedral of Constance, and will give a ducat to all who are present. We are at present entirely at liberty in the town. The Master officiates every day, and acts everywhere freely. He does not keep at a distance from the king's council, that, in the cause of truth, which is also his own, nothing may be undertaken against him before the arrival of the King of Hungary.* The Council has not yet taken the affair into consideration; up to this time there has not arrived any ambassador from the king or prince, neither from Gregory nor Benedict; and we do not think the Council will open its sittings before several weeks. Let all those who are personally cited be careful of themselves, and know well that their names are publicly affixed to the church-doors. Michael Causis chants his high deeds. The Seigniors John Lepka and Wenceslaus of Lesma are the intrepid and zealous defenders of the truth.†

[Written at Constance on the Sunday before Saint Martin's day.]

---

* The King of Hungary, to whom John of Janowitz here alludes, is Sigismund, the second son of Charles IV., and brother of Wenceslaus, King of Bohemia. This prince succeeded Robert to the imperial throne; and the distinguished part he took in the Council of Constance is well known. At that period he had not yet been crowned, and was usually only designated by the titles of *King of Hungary*, and *King of the Romans*, although he was, in fact, Emperor. To avoid all confusion, we have already given him his imperial title, and shall continue doing so throughout.

† John of Janowitz terminates his letter with the following *jeu de*

LETTER V.

JOHN HUSS TO THE PEOPLE OF BOHEMIA AND HIS
FRIENDS.

Salutation through Jesus Christ. We entered Constance after the festival of All-Saints' day, without having suffered injury in the towns we passed through, and where we delivered public discourses in Latin and German. We lodge at Constance, in the Great Square, near the Pope's hotel; and we have arrived without a safe-conduct.* The next day, Michael Causis stuck up a notice on the church, containing an accusation against me; he affixed his signature to it, with a long commentary, which indicated, amongst other things, that this accusation was directed against the obstinate John Huss, excommunicated and suspected of heresy. I endeavour, with God's aid, not to pay attention to it, knowing that God has created him my enemy on account of my sins, in order to judge whether I am willing or able to suffer something for his name's sake.

mots :—" Auca nondum est assata, nec timet de assatione, quia præsenti anno, sabbato ante Martini festum, occurrit ipsius celebris vigilia, ubi ante non comeduntur.

    * Without a safe-conduct from the Pope. See Letter VI.

Lutzembock and John of Lepka have visited the Pope, and spoken to him about me : he answered, that he did not wish to resort to violent measures. It is rumoured, though vaguely, that Pope Benedict is coming from Spain to be present at the Council. We have learned to-day, that the Dukes of Brabant and Burgundy have withdrawn from the camp. The Pope and the Council must wait for the Emperor, who is to be crowned at Aix ; and as this town is seventy miles distant from Constance, I do not think the Emperor can be here before Christmas ; the Council will be then near its close, unless it is broken up about Easter. The living here is exceedingly expensive, a bed costing half a florin a-week. Horses are at a high price, and seven florins are paid for a horse that might be bought in Bohemia for six drachms. The Seignior John and myself have sent ours to the town of Ravensburg, four miles from here, and I think I shall not be long before I shall want common necessaries. Mention my uneasiness to our friends, whom it would take too long to name severally. The Seignior Lutzembock has gone to-day to rejoin the Emperor, and has probibited me from undertaking any thing before the arrival of Sigismund. I hope I shall answer before a public audience. Many Italians and Parisians are here, but few bishops and archbishops : the cardinals, also, are numerous. When I traversed Constance on horseback, I was surrounded by a large crowd of horsemen, and the multitude pressed round me. Our Bohemians have spent all their money on the road, and are already in want. I pity greatly their distress, but I cannot give to all. I have only kept my horse Robstein, the swiftest horse here, and which I guard, in case I should wish to leave this city, and rejoin the Emperor. Salute our friends, without excepting any one. This letter is the fourth I write from a foreign country, and I date it, Sunday night after All-Saints' day. Not one of our Bohemian knights is at Constance, with the exception of the Seignior John Lepka, who has protected and conducted me like a true knight. He preaches more than I do, and proclaims everywhere my innocence. Pray to God to sustain my courage.

JOHN HUSS, servant of God in hope.

LETTER VI.

Know, my well-beloved friends, that I am well in every respect. I have arrived at Constance without any safe-conduct from the Pope. Pray, then, to God that he may grant me firmness; for many and redoubtable adversaries rise up here against me, excited especially by the seller of indulgences, the Deacon of Padua, and Michael Causis,

who are unceasingly plotting against me. Nevertheless, I
fear them not, being in hope that, after a great combat
will come a great victory, and after the victory my reward, and the confusion of my persecutors.

The Pope will not put an end to the affair : " What
can I do?" says he ; " it is you who are to act." Two
bishops, however, and a doctor, have conversed with John
Lepka, that we might agree without noise. I conceive
they are afraid that I should answer in public, but I hope
I shall be permitted to do so when the Emperor is
present.

We have been well received, and honourably treated in
all the towns we have passed through, and we have published declarations* in Latin and German. In the imperial towns we held discussions with the masters. The
Bishop of Lubeck, who preceded us, and was a night in
advance of us, reported everywhere on the road that I
was conducted in chains, in a cart ; and told the people
he kept aloof from me, because I seduced the minds of
men. In consequence, whenever we approached a town,
the crowd ran to meet us, as if to a show. But this falsehood has turned to the confusion of my enemies, and the
people rejoiced on learning the truth. Truly Jesus
Christ is with me, like a valiant warrior, and I defy all
the power of my enemies. Live purely, and pray fer-

---

* Intimationes.

vently, that the God of mercy may assist me, and defend, through me, his Word.

Written on Saint Leonard's eve.

I think, should the Council be prolonged, I shall want for common necessaries : ask, therefore, for some assistance for me, but only under condition agreed on, from those whom you discover to be really my friends. Salute our brethren and sisters, and invite them to pray to God for me, since I am in need of it.

LETTER VII.

.TO THE PEOPLE OF BOHEMIA.

May the grace and peace of our Lord Jesus Christ be with you, so that, being delivered from sin, you may walk in grace, increase in modesty and virtue, and enjoy, after this life, life eternal!

My well-beloved, I conjure you all who live according to God's law, disdain not to occupy yourselves with the salvation of souls : be careful, when listening to the word of God, that you are not deceived by false apostles, who do not condemn sins, but who excuse them : they flatter the priests : they do not shew to the people their transgressions : they glorify themselves, extol their works, and exalt their own virtue ; but they deign not to imitate Jesus Christ in his humility, in his poverty, in his cross, in his sufferings.   It is of them our merciful Saviour has said—" False Christs and false prophets shall rise, and deceive many."   And to warn his elect against them, he has said to them, " Beware of false prophets, which come to you in sheep's clothing, but inwardly they are ravening wolves ; ye shall know them by their fruits." And truly the followers of Christ have the greatest need to be prudent and careful ; for the Saviour has said, " insomuch that if it were possible they shall deceive the very elect."   Watch, therefore, my beloved, through fear of falling into the snares of Satan.   It is necessary you should be the more circumspect in proportion as Antichrist places in your way greater obstacles.   The last judgment is nigh, death will swallow up many, but the kingdom of God is waiting for his elect, since for them he delivered up his body.   Fear not death ; love one another ; and endeavour, without ceasing, to understand the will of God.   Let the terrible and formidable day of judgment be present ever before your eyes, for fear that you may sin ; think also of the joys of eternal life, to which all your efforts should be directed ; think also of the passion of our Saviour, that you may bear with humility all things with him and for him ; for if you bear in mind his sufferings and his cross, nothing will appear too rigorous for you; you will accept, without murmurings, tribulations, calumnies, outrages, chains; and, should it be required, you will not hesitate to lay down your life for the holy truth. Know, dearly-beloved, that Antichrist has recourse, in his rage against you, to divers persecutions; but he has been powerless against a great number; he has not been able even to remove a single hair from their heads; learn to know him by my example, although he is violently irritated against me. Wherefore, I conjure you all to intercede for me in your prayers at the throne of God, that he may grant me wisdom, mildness, patience, as well as strength, to keep always in the heavenly truth. It is that which has already conducted me to Constance; and during the whole journey I have publicly and openly declared my name, as became a servant of God. Nowhere did I conceal myself; but in no place have I found more dangerous or declared enemies than in this city; and I should not have had them for adversaries, if some Bohemian impostors, for the money which they had received, and seduced by avarice, had not persuaded them that I mislead the people from the good way. But I have good hope, by the mercy of our Saviour and your prayers, that I shall persevere until death in the immutable truth of our Heavenly Father.

Know, lastly, that every one here has his duty assigned him; I alone am neglected. It is the Pope who has regulated every thing here. I recommend myself to our sweet Lord Jesus Christ, to the true God, to the Son of the Virgin Mary, who ransomed us by a bitter death, and not through our merits, from eternal punishment, from the power of the devil and sin.

On Saint Fabin's eve (January 19), written at Constance, 1415.

LETTER VIII.

TO THE INHABITANTS OF PRAGUE.

[Huss conjures them to remember his doctrines, and to cling to the Word of God.]

May God be with you ! I conjure you, dearly-beloved, to attach yourselves to the cause of the Lord ; for several endeavour to stifle the word, and take away from you the Gospel of Christ, which I have preached unto you, in order to turn men from their salvation. Reflect, in the second place, on the slights and outrages which your nation inflicts on you ;—which hypocrites wickedly excite against you ; think of the infamies and insults heaped upon you ; in a word, support all things with joy and patience.

If Satan insults you, if Antichrist holds you in derision, he cannot harm you more than a dog tied-up, as long as you love the Word of God and defend it with all your power. Look at me! Satan has persecuted me for some years past, but he has not been able to do me any harm, because I trust in God. I will even say more, God strengthens in me every day joy and contentment. Remember also, that to deny a thing, is to abjure what one believes, be it the true faith or a heresy. If a man is a Christian, and if, through fear of death or persecution, and seduced by the wiles of the demon, he joins the sect of Jews and Pagans, and declares on oath that he does not wish to be a Christian, he denies the true faith. But if another has adopted a heresy; if, for example, he does not believe Jesus Christ to be God; if, in the end, he abjures this opinion, it cannot be said of him that he persists in his error. Acknowledging, therefore, how much he sins who denies the truth when he has once come to a knowledge of it, or who adheres to error or heresy, and esteeming more than all, the Word of God, let us celebrate his glory above all things, and live in charity with all men. Wrestle courageously against the imposture of Antichrist, having with you your Saviour, who strengthens you, and whom no one can vanquish. He will not forsake you, if you do not forsake him; but will bestow on all the faithful who believe in him, an eternal reward. I wrote these things, not being able to come to you in person—1415.

LETTER IX.

[John Huss to a priest, whom he reminds of his duties.]

My very dear Brother,—Be zealous in preaching the Scriptures, fill the office of a good preacher of the Gospel, remember thy vocation, and work like a favoured soldier of Christ. Live, first of all, piously and purely; afterwards, teach faithfully and sincerely. Be unto others an example in every good work; leave nothing to be desired in thy discourses; recommend virtue, and bring back those who live wickedly to the remembrance of eternal punishment; point out the joys of heaven to those who live in faith and piety; preach assiduously but briefly; explain, lastly, the Holy Scriptures prudently and with profit. Take heed of affirming any thing uncertain and doubtful, for fear of being taken up by adversaries who delight to find their neighbour in fault, and bring contempt on God's ministers; exhort to confession and to the Communion of the Body and Blood of Jesus Christ, under both forms, that those who sincerely repent of their sins may often communicate.

I exhort thee, dear brother, not to frequent taverns or strangers, in order not to live like the common run of men; for the more the priest keeps aloof from public places, and dissïpation, the more he is acceptable to God. Nevertheless, refuse not thine assistance to others, according to thy means. Preach with all thy might against voluptuousness; it is a wild beast that devours men, for whom the humanity of Christ has suffered. Wherefore, my dear friend, I conjure you to avoid all impurity; for even when thou shalt most endeavour to be useful, temptation will conceal itself, in order to lay hold of thee. Shun entirely the company of young women, and trust not to their devotion. Saint Augustin has said: "*Quo religiosior, eo ad luxuriam proclivior, et sub prætextu religionis latet dolus aut venenum fornicationis.*" Know, my dear friend, that their society has seduced many, whom the life of the age has not destroyed. Introduce not, under any pretext, women into thy dwelling, and do not hold too frequent intercourse with them; lastly, whatever thou doest, fear God, and keep his commandments, for so thou shalt be in the right path; thou shalt not perish, but shalt curb thy flesh, master the world, vanquish the demon, put on a divine spirit, find life, strengthen others, and place on thy own head a crown of glory, which shall be given thee, by the equitable and sovereign Dispenser of all justice.

LETTER X.*

TO PETER MALDONIEWITZ.

[John Huss wrote the following letters in the prison where he was first detained, at the Monastery of the Minor Brothers, near the Lake of Constance, outside the city walls.]

I have written nothing at present on my captivity except the letter, if, indeed, thou hast sent it, in which I besought to be prayed for. Thou understandest, without doubt, that I allude to the letter I addressed to Master Jacobel, and in which I wrote: " My enemies have said that I shall not obtain an audience, unless I, first of all, pay two thousand ducats to the ministers of Antichrist for their expenses."† Michael‡ has brought a copy of this letter, and the answer of Master Jacobel, which, I have reason to believe, is severe for me. He came with the patriarch, accompanied by scribes and witnesses, amongst whom was Master Nicholas. Stoggis stood up right in front of me. One of the commissioners handing me the copy to read over, asked me to declare on

* This is the 43d in the collection of John Huss's Works.
† The letter thus alluded to has not come down to us.
‡ Michael Causis.

oath if it was mine. I answered; Yes, and I do not believe, since the cruel salutations of Master Paletz, that any thing troubled me more than these letters. I shudder at the wickedness of Michael, and of his accomplices. As to Master Jacobel, who preaches that we should beware of hypocrites, he is deceived by them more than any one, and delivers himself up to them. I have not read his letter, but I believe it to be severe. There were two copies in the same paper, and I thought at first it was not an answer to mine, but a copy of the letter of the Curé of Janowitz.

LETTER XI.

TO THE BELIEVERS IN PRAGUE.

[A letter written from Constance, by John Huss, to the community of Prague, during the early part of his imprisonment.*]

May God be with you; so that, in wrestling against Satan and the world, you may persevere to the end. I

---

* This letter was read at Prague, in the Chapel of Bethlehem, and in the other churches.

conjure you, well-beloved, from the prison which I in-
habit, to pray to God for me, who do not blush to bear
affliction for him : pray that he may assist me ; for all
my life lies in him, and your prayers. Beseech him,
therefore, to grant his Spirit unto me, that I may confess his name, even unto death. I cling to his mercy and
truth ; and if at this time he deign to receive me, let his
holy will be done ! But if it be his will I should live
and be restored to you, let his holy will again be blessed.
I shall be in need of his Divine assistance, although I
am assured that he will not permit me to be tried beyond my strength, and exposed to a peril that will not
ensure my salvation and yours ; for the end of temptation, should we hold fast in the truth, is to effect our
salvation. Know, dearly-beloved, that the letters I have
left you, have been translated by my adversaries, who
have added to them many falsehoods. They write so
many articles and lies against me, that I have enough to
do to answer them from my prison. Their malice equals
their fury. Jesus Christ, our merciful Lord, has said to
them whom he loved, " I will give you a mouth and wisdom, which all your adversaries shall not be able to gainsay nor resist." Remember, beloved, that I have never
had anything more at heart from the beginning than
your salvation ; it is in his name that I have taught you
the Word of God, and I shall never cease doing so, even

from the bottom of my prison. I do not doubt but that you will make some mention of me.

[Written on the eve before St Fabin's day.]

LETTER XII.*

TO JOHN OF CHLUM.

[He exhorts him not to depart, as likewise his friends, before the end of the trial.]

Excellent Lord, I rejoice greatly at your good health, your presence here, and the firm perseverance of your good and faithful heart in the trouble which you take for me in my misfortunes. God has given you that constancy to a higher degree than to any other person; he bestows you on me for my support, and I hope it will be for your welfare in this life and in the next.

I beseech you, then, by the mercy of God, to wait for the termination of the affair, like a soldier of Jesus Christ. If the Seignior John of Janowitz, who lived with us, is in good health, I ask you to keep him also near you.

* *Hist. et Monum. Johann. Huss*, Epist. li.

I think often with pleasure of the noble Seignior Wenceslaus Duba. I pray you to transmit to him, saluting him from me, what I say of him in my prison, and thank him for his undeviating fidelity. Salute also all the other faithful Bohemians.

I accuse myself, that, on the unexpected appearance of Master Christian, my faithful master and benefactor, I could not restrain the tears which flowed from my eyes.

I was told you had left some time since with all your suite, but my soul is comforted. The God of all goodness at one time consoles, at another afflicts me; but I hope he will not forsake me in my trials. I have again suffered horribly from the stone, from which I had never suffered previously to my imprisonment; I have also been attacked by fever, and seized with vomitings, and my jailors, who took me out of the prison, thought I should have died here.

There are now presented to me many articles, heaps of falsehoods, besides those concerning which you have already received many answers. I have not dared reply to the writing which you transmitted to me, on the subject of the articles of the Parisian Doctors; for I could not do it secretly, being closely watched. It is better for me to abstain, rather than place in peril this faithful friend whom I recommend to you.*

* John Huss speaks twice in this letter of a friend whom he does not name.

I would willingly see you with the Seignior Wenceslaus and Master Christian. If you speak to the vice-chamberlain, I think he will permit you to be admitted. Converse before my guards in Latin. . . . . . . I did not dare keep the articles about my person. Make Peter copy what I have written on the Ten Commandments of God.

If I live I will answer the articles of the Chancellor of Paris ;* if I die, God will answer them for me at the day of judgment.

I know not where is my faithful brother in Christ. Is Master Christian with you ? I pray you salute him, as likewise the Seignior Wenceslaus, and the other faithful Bohemians.†

Torment not yourself about the living being dear here. ‚Live as you can; and should God permit me to leave the prison, you will not repent these expenses.

If you see the Seignior Henry of Plumlovitz, or Stibor of Botz, salute them for me.

It will be eight weeks to-morrow that John Huss has been confined in this refectory.‡

---

* John Gerson. Huss adds,—Scribet in manifesto *Zeleznyian.* The meaning of this latter word is not clear.

† John Huss here repeats what he had said in a former part of this letter, which is written in Latin, and is often very obscure, indicating a certain derangement, occasioned, without doubt, by acute sufferings.

‡ In the refectory of the Minor Brothers. The date of this letter is thus fixed as 22d January 1415.

Noble and good Seignior, and defender of the truth,
remain here with constancy, you and the Seignior Henry,
until the end arrives ; and I hope that our Saviour Jesus
Christ will permit it to contribute to his glory and to the
ransom of my sins.

I should behold with pleasure the Emperor command-
ing me to transmit him my answers on the articles of
Wycliffe.   Oh ! if God would deign to put wisdom in his
mouth, that he might comport himself amongst the princes
as the defender of the truth !

I have finished to-day an essay on the Body of Christ ;
yesterday I wrote another on Marriage.   You will get
them copied.   Some Polish knights, and a single Bohemian in their company, have visited me.

LETTER XIII.*

TO THE SAME.

[John Huss, so many times and so perfidiously questioned by his
    adversaries, declares again what he acquiesces in.]

Noble and good Seignior, I have great consolation experienced, and I implore you in the name of God not to

* *Hist. et Monum. Johann. Huss*, Epist. lii.

lose patience in taking so much trouble about me for so long a time; the God of truth and of justice will reward you for it.

The Commissioners during several days wished to confide my affair to twelve or thirteen head lawyers. I refused to consent to it. But, after having written my answers to the forty-five articles of Wycliffe, as well as to those of my own, which are alleged against me, I wrote with my own hand a protest, by which I declared that I wished to appear before the whole Council, and there uphold my faith. In it will be seen the articles which have been falsely extracted from my treatise on *The Church*, being added to and taken from, as well as the answer which I wrote in prison, without the assistance of any book.

I have never in my life found in my misfortune a more cruel comforter than Paletz.

All the clerks of the Pope's chamber, as well as my keepers, treat me with great attention. The Lord delivered Jonas from the belly of the whale; Daniel from the lion's den; the three young men from the fiery furnace: and Susanna from the sentence of false witnesses; he can also deliver me, if it should promote his glory and the preaching of his word; if, on the contrary, my death is agreeable to the Lord, let God's name be blessed. If, at least, I was permitted to see only once the Emperor with our Bohemians, I should be consoled in my affliction.

I rejoiced in the news which I have received; truly

the Lord has comforted me. I was happy to hear of the Seignior Henry Snopek being in good health. I wish to have a Bible sent me. Do not grieve on my account. I conjure you to treat well this faithful friend, to whom I am under particular obligations.

LETTER XIV.*

TO THE SAME.

[Huss desires to have several things in his prison to beguile the
time, and fortify himself by the perusal of the Holy Scriptures.]

My good Seignior, endeavour to obtain a Bible for me, and send it by this excellent man ;† and if Peter, your secretary, has any ink, let him give me some, with a few pens and an inkstand.

I have no news of my Polish servant, nor of Master Cardinal; I have learned only that your noblemen are here with the Emperor; wherefore, I conjure you to entreat his Majesty in my favour, and in the name of Almighty

* *Hist. et Monum. Johan. Huss*, Epist. liii.

† Huss transmits, without doubt, this message by one of the keepers, whom he praises in another letter.

God, who has so generously bestowed his gifts upon him, and on account of the justice and truth which ought to be made manifest for the honour of God and the advancement of his Church ; beseech his Majesty to deliver me from my chains, that I may be enabled to dispose of myself, and appear before a public assembly. Learn that I have been very ill, and have been obliged to take remedies, but that I am now better. Salute, I pray you, the Bohemian noblemen who are at the King's court.

*Written in prison, and by the well-known hand of Peter our secretary.**

LETTER XV.†

TO THE SAME.

[He exhorts his friends to beware of the snares of his adversaries, who, like the Corycæans, listen to and envenom all things.]‡

I have passed nearly the whole of last night in answering in writing the articles that Paletz has drawn up ;

* Peter Maldoniewitz.

† *Hist. et Monum. Johann. Huss*, Epist. liv.

‡ Luther adds : "*Male loquentes etiam Cardinali Hostiensi.*" He is deceived when he takes the Cardinal Osti for Master John Cardinal, referred to in this letter : the latter was a Doctor of Prague, and a friend of John Huss. The manner in which Huss expresses himself on this subject, suffices to shew Luther's error.

E

he labours directly for the purpose of procuring my condemnation. May God pardon him, and be my aid!

They affirm that the article concerning the depriving the clergy of their property is heretical. Make the Emperor understand that if this article is condemned as a heresy, it will follow that he himself, as well as his father the Emperor and King of Bohemia,* will be condemned as heretics, for having stripped the bishops of temporal wealth. Do not send a letter by any one whom you cannot answer for as for yourself.

Tell Doctor Schmitz to beware of coming here, or Master Jerome, or any of our friends.

I am astonished that the Emperor has forgotten me, and does not communicate with me. Perhaps I shall be condemned before I have said a word to him. It is for him to see if it is to his honour to act thus.

Noble and good Seignior John, my excellent benefactor, my intrepid defender, I conjure you not to let yourself be troubled on my account, nor for the losses from which you suffer; Almighty God will reward you with usury. Salute, I pray you, our Bohemian Lords; I do not know any thing concerning them, but I think that the Seignior Wenceslaus Duba is here, as well as Henry Latzembock.

If you decide upon any thing, let me know of it. Let

---

* The Emperor Charles IV.

John Bradazk, who is so dear to me, pray to God, with all the others, for me, and cause the Emperor to ask for the answers signed by my hand; those I have drawn up for the articles of Wycliffe, as well as for those imputed to myself.

Let these answers be copied, but not shewn more than is necessary, and let the copies not be too much multiplied, in order that the articles may remain quite distinct. I know not if the petition will be read which I forwarded to the Patriarch, to lay before the Council. I think he will not present it. If it pleased God, the Emperor, by means of one or two articles, might reduce to nothing the conclusions of the Doctors of Prague, concerning the subtraction of property, the donation of Constantine, and alms. I did not wish to deny these articles. It would be necessary for the Emperor to allege some good motives, and that these were suggested to him by some one who is not one of ours. If I was free, I would speak alone with the Emperor. See him, in order that the affair which concerns you, and to which you are attached, should not be secretly transferred elsewhere, to prevent your interfering in it any longer.

Let Master John Cardinal be prudent, for those he imagines to be friends are spies; and I have heard it said by several of those who questioned me, A certain John Cardinal has confounded together the Pope and the Cardinals, in saying that they were all simonists. Let

Master Cardinal keep as much as possible under the imperial roof, that his person may not be seized as mine was.* No one has done me so much harm as Paletz. May God forgive him! Paletz has directed everything. He insisted upon citing all the persons who adhered to my opinions, that they might be constrained to abjure. He has said, in my prison, that all those who came to hear me, maintained that the material bread remained after consecration.

I am surprised none of our Bohemians visit my prison; perhaps they act all for the best. Let this paper be torn directly after it is read.

Send by the bearer of this letter another shirt. Seignior John, insist with the Bohemians, that the citation of all those who are called upon to appear, may be annulled; that the Emperor may consider his heritage, and not suffer any ill-disposed person to harm it. Why can I not speak to him once before being condemned? for I came here after his desire, and with the promise that I should be permitted to return safe and sound to Bohemia.

---

* This alone is sufficient to prove that the person in question was not Cardinal Osti, President of the Council.

LETTER XVI.*

TO THE SAME.

[He informs his friends of Pope John's flight, and requests the Bohemian Nobles to employ their efforts to obtain his deliverance.]

My keepers have already taken themselves away. I am no longer supplied with food, and I am ignorant of the fate that awaits me in my prison. I implore you to go with the other Nobles to the Emperor, to induce him to put an end to my captivity, that he fall not, on account of me, into sin and confusion. I beseech you also to come and see me with our Nobles of Bohemia, for it is necessary that I should speak with you.

Noble Seignior John, go and speedily find the Emperor with the Seignior Wenceslaus and all the others; it would be dangerous to wait: it is important for me that it should be done as soon as possible. Come quickly, and learn the other things which I desire you to do.

I fear that the Grand Master of the Papal Court may carry me away with him this night, for he has remained

---

* *Hist. et Monum. Johann. Huss*, Epist. lvi.

to-day at the monastery.   The Bishop of Constance has written to me that he would not treat any affair with me.   The cardinals have done the same.

If you love the unfortunate Huss,* take care the king gives me guards of his own court, and that he delivers me from prison this evening.

Written in prison on Sunday evening.

My noble lord, delay not!

LETTER XVII.†

TO THE SAME.

[He tells him of the consolation which he has received in prison.]

I have received great consolation from the visit of the Bohemian noblemen, but I was much distressed at not having been permitted to see you.‡   Master Christian has left the city, bearing the message of Seignior Henry,

* Si diligitis miserum anserem.
† *Hist. et Monum. Johann. Huss,* Epist. lv.
‡ The regret thus expressed by Huss would lead to the presumption that this letter, like the preceding, was addressed to John of Chlum, whose name is not found among those of the Seigniors and friends of John Huss, mentioned by the latter as having visited him in prison.

and also of Master Jessenitz. I think the Council is much agitated on account of the Pope's flight.

In all things executed, or to be executed, God should be consulted before human reason. This is what they have not done, and it is why*

* * * * * * *

If God grants me a happy issue I will not forget this faithful friend ;† but if my death is only deferred, it is to you I recommend him.

I have discovered that the Seignior William is my friend ; return him thanks for me.

I saw Wenceslaus Duba shedding tears when he spoke to me, and the Seignior Mozka shewed me all the kindness of a friend.

LETTER XVIII.‡

JOHN HUSS TO HIS BENEFACTORS.

[He returns them thanks; exhorts them to live purely; and reminds them of the conduct of the Council towards Pope John XXIII. after his flight.]

Most generous Lords, faithful defenders of the truth, and my consolers; you whom God has sent as angels to

---

* Here the text is deficient.

† It is probable that this friend, whom he does not name, is the one to whom he has already alluded in several preceding letters.

‡ *Hist. et Monum. Johann. Huss*, Epist. xix.

me, I cannot fully express to you how grateful I feel for
all the constancy and charitable kindness that you have
shewn to me a poor sinner, but a servant in the hope of
our Lord Jesus Christ.   I trust the Divine Jesus, our
Creator, Redeemer, and Saviour, will reward you in the
present life, and give himself unto you, as the most precious gift in the life to come.   I exhort you, therefore,
by his mercy, to bind yourselves strongly to his law and
holy commandments.

Noble Lord Wenceslaus, in taking a spouse, live purely
in marriage, and renounce the vanities of the age; and
you, Lord John of Chlum, you who already serve no
longer the kings of the earth, dwell with your wife and
your children under the yoke of the Lord.

You behold how the wheel of the vanities of the world
turns round, raising one man and depressing another, but
giving to all whom it raises a fleeting joy; after which
comes the eternal punishment in fire and darkness.

You know of what description are these spiritual
princes who call themselves the true vicars of Christ and
his Apostles; who proclaim themselves the Holy Church,
and the very Sacred Council that is infallible; and which,
nevertheless, transgressed in adoring John XXIII., and
in calling him most holy, when they knew him to be a
manslayer, impure, a simonist, and a heretic, as they
have declared him to be in the sentence which condemns
him.   Behold how they have struck off the head of the

Church ; they have torn out the heart of the Church ; they have dried up the inexhaustible fountain of the Church ; they have violated and destroyed the imperishable refuge of the Church, where every Christian should find a refuge!

May God pardon Stanislaus, Paletz, and their brethren ; for they thus designated the Pope in the sentence which they rendered by the mouth of Stanislaus.*

     *   *   *   *   *

And now Christendom is without a Pope ; it has Jesus Christ for the Head, who directs it—for the heart that vivifies it by grace—for the fountain which waters it with the seven gifts of the Holy Ghost—for the imperishable and never-failing refuge, to which I have recourse in my misfortune, in the firm hope that there I shall always find direction, assistance, and an all-sufficient regeneration, and that God will fill me with infinite joy, by delivering me from my sins, and from this miserable life !

The Council erred several times in erroneously rejecting some articles from my books, as tainted with corruption, and mutilating several passages, as will be seen on comparing these articles with my books. It is there evident to both of us that Jesus Christ, the infallible Judge, will not sanction all that has been done and said at this Council. Happy, then, are they who,

* John Huss repeats again here what he had previously said relative to the Pope. We omit it as superfluous.

keeping his law, perceive, detest, and avoid vain pomp, avarice, hypocrisy, the fraud of Christ's enemies, and who wait with patience the coming of the Sovereign Judge and his angels.

I conjure you, by the bowels of Jesus Christ, to avoid bad priests, and to love good ones, according to their works. I conjure you and the faithful Barons, not to permit, according to your power, worthy priests to be oppressed. It is for that purpose that God has raised you above others ; and I think there will be in Bohemia a great persecution of the faithful servants of God, if he does not relieve them by the arms of the secular lords whom he has enlightened by his Word, more than by our spiritual chiefs. Oh! what madness to condemn as erroneous the Gospel of Christ and the Epistle of St Paul, who professes to have received the truth, not from men, but from God ; and to reject the example of Jesus Christ himself, of his apostles, and of the other saints, in condemning the Communion of the Cup of our Lord, instituted for all adult believers. Do they not say, the permission given to devout laymen to participate with the lips in the Cup of Christ is an error! And if a priest presents them this Cup to drink of, he is reputed in fault, and, should he persist, is condemned as a heretic!

O, St Paul, thou hast said unto all the faithful—" For as often as ye eat this bread, and drink this cup, ye do shew the Lord's death till he come," that is to say, until the judgment-day, when he shall come; and, behold, already the custom of the Romish Church opposes the accomplishment of thy Word!

LETTER XIX.*

TO JOHN OF CHLUM.

[He alludes to the injuries which he had to suffer from the Council and deputies.]

If my letter has not yet been sent to Bohemia, keep it, and do not send it, for harm might come from it.

The Emperor might well ask who was to be judge, since the Council has not cited me to appear before him, nor have I been accused in his presence. Nevertheless, the Council has cast me into prison, and ordered its procurator to proceed against me.

If I obtain a public audience, I ask, noble and excellent Seignior John, that the Emperor should be present, and a place near him assigned to me, in order that he may hear me with facility. I also pray, that you, with the

* *Hist. et Monum. Johann. Huss*, Epist. xlix.

Master Cardinal keep as much as possible under the imperial roof, that his person may not be seized as mine was.* No one has done me so much harm as Paletz. May God forgive him! Paletz has directed everything. He insisted upon citing all the persons who adhered to my opinions, that they might be constrained to abjure. He has said, in my prison, that all those who came to hear me, maintained that the material bread remained after consecration.

I am surprised none of our Bohemians visit my prison; perhaps they act all for the best. Let this paper be torn directly after it is read.

Send by the bearer of this letter another shirt. Seignior John, insist with the Bohemians, that the citation of all those who are called upon to appear, may be annulled; that the Emperor may consider his heritage, and not suffer any ill-disposed person to harm it. Why can I not speak to him once before being condemned? for I came here after his desire, and with the promise that I should be permitted to return safe and sound to Bohemia.

---

* This alone is sufficient to prove that the person in question was ~~Cardinal Osti,~~ President of the Council.

lehem, and I with them; and on awaking, I found that I was laughing.

Several have published, that they wished to destroy what is written at Bethlehem. I will send a copy of the treatises, which I have transcribed in duplicate.

LETTER XXI.*

PETER MALDONIEWITZ TO JOHN HUSS.

[Peter explains the dream to John Huss, according to the interpretation of John of Chlum, whom, in pleasantry, they used to call the Doctor of Bibrach; because, during John Huss's stay in the imperial town of Bibrach, as John of Chlum frequently conferred with the priests and other lettered men, relative to the obedience due to the Pope, excommunication, and other similar matters, the report was disseminated in the town, that the nobleman, John of Chlum, had been created Doctor in Theology.]

Dearest friend, Be not in any respect uneasy respecting the public audience, for it occupies more attention than usual, as well as your affairs; and we hope, with the grace of God, that every thing will terminate happily.

* *Hist. et Monum. Johann. Huss*, Epist., xlv.

But trouble not your head with phantoms; forget them, and think only in what manner you may reply to the objections that will be made against you. And yet the word of truth, which cannot err, forbids you to meditate too much; for it declares, that when you are brought before men, it shall be suggested to you at the moment what you ought to say.

This is the explanation of your dream:—The image of Christ, painted on the walls of the chapel, is his life, which we ought to imitate; it is the same for the holy and ineffaceable Scripture which is represented on the same place, and which, towards the evening, the enemies of the cross endeavour to rub out, the sun withdrawing itself from them on account of the iniquities of their life; all these things, then, appear forgotten in the eyes of the world; but the next day, when the sun of justice shall have risen again, the preachers of Christ's word will renew these same images, and will retrace them in a more brilliant manner, then preaching on the house-tops what was before only whispered in the ear, and, as it were, delivered up to oblivion. The result will be a great source of joy to believers; and although the humble bird, * at present placed on the altar, may be delivered up to suffering in putting off a feeble body; yet our firm hope is, that hereafter awakening, after this miserable life, as from a dream, it will live with Him who is in

* Auca, *goose*, the signification of *Huss* in Bohemia.

Heaven, and will laugh to scorn those impious persons, who endeavoured to destroy the image of Christ and the Holy Scriptures ; and that at the last with the divine protection, he will again, in a more remarkable manner, retrace the latter, for his flock and his dear friends. This is the explanation given by the Doctor of Bibrach,* in comparing this dream with one of Daniel's visions.

     *   *   *   *   *   *   *

Your friends and faithful disciples are happy in receiving your letters. The Ambassador of the King of France has arrived to-day at Constance.

---

* Peter adds, " Correspondenter hunc locum visionis Danielis exponens conformiter illi ; quo auca in mari natitans petræ inniti videbatur, quorum utrumque inconvulsam sustentaminis innuit firmitatem."

LETTER XXII.*

REPLY OF JOHN HUSS TO PETER.

[He explains his dream himself, and comforts himself by the
Holy Scriptures.]

I have received much consolation from what the Doctor
of Bibrach has desired you to write to me; his explanation is in accordance with my own ideas. I forget
neither this precept of Cato—" Disturb not thyself with
dreams ;" nor the order of God—" Pay not observance to
visions ;" and yet I hope that the life of Christ, which I
imprinted at Bethlehem by his word in the hearts of my
hearers, and which his enemies have endeavoured to destroy, by forbidding me to preach in that place, and by
wishing to pull it down,—I hope, I say, that this same
life shall be sketched hereafter far more effectively by
preachers of greater eloquence than myself, to the great
joy of the people who cling with all their might to the
life of Christ; greatly shall I rejoice when I awake, as
our Doctor expresses it,—that is to say, when I shall
rise from the bosom of the dead !

And as to the Scripture printed on the walls of Bethlehem, and relative to which Paletz is so much irritated,
declaring that I have abused the people about it, this

* *Hist. et Monum. Johann. Huss*, Epist. xlvi.

same Paletz insists on its being destroyed; and in order to overwhelm me as much as possible, he has greeted me in a most dreadful manner, as I shall relate hereafter, with God's permission.

With respect to what I ought to reply to the objections that may be brought against me, I rely on the Divine Saviour, to whom I have appealed—whom, in presence of the commissioners, I have chosen for my Judge and Advocate, declaring firmly, that "I selected for my advocate and judge the Lord Jesus, him who would soon judge us all." I committed my cause to him, as he had confided his to his Father. It is he who has declared, as our doctoral lord of Bibrach remarks,—" Take no heed of what you shall say; for I will give you a wisdom and eloquence which your enemies will not be able to resist."

Jerome has written :—" The Lord has said to us, Do not allow yourselves to be troubled; fear nothing; you shall march to the combat, but it is I who will fight; your mouth shall open, but it is I who will speak; you shall be betrayed by your relations, your friends, your brothers; and they will deliver you up to death. The injuries that we receive from the persons who are strangers to us are less cruel than others; our sufferings are so much the more bitter, that we expected more from those who inflicted them on us; for we suffer not only in our body, but also in our mind, from charity being destroyed."

This is what Jerome says; and as to me, my grief proceeds, above all, from Paletz.

In truth, the Doctor of Bibrach has the advantage over Lord Henry, and over Master John of Janowitz. The other dreams will be also explained, if it please God.*

Let the Doctor of Bibrach keep to himself alone what he has imparted to me, relative to my letters; for Christ has said,—" A man's enemies are of his own household, and you shall be betrayed by your own relatives."

Farewell! Be firm and constant all you that dwell in this city of Constance.† Greet all my friends for me, but prudently, for fear the question be asked, How you know that I have sent them a greeting?

LETTER XXIII.‡

TO JOHN HUSS.

[Huss is informed of several circumstances by his friends.]

Dearest friend,—Learn that your acts and the truth have never been more the objects of secret and unjustifiable

* The Latin text has the word cætera; but it is probable that dreams are meant.

† Habete constantiam in Constantia omnes qui simul estis.

‡ Hist. et Monum. Johann. Huss, Epist. l.

snares than at present; however, your affair is postponed in consequence of a train of incidents that have occurred, and which were not in any way connected with it.

All your friends, and particularly Christian, are most attentive to the good widow, as to a second Sareptan.*

A bit of triangular paper has fallen into the hands of your enemies: it has been the subject of a denunciation; and the informations were lodged so promptly, that it was impossible to prevent the act.

The Doctor of Bibrach has been demanding, by what means, and by what occasion, he can write to you: the conclusion that has been drawn, is, that he is negligent about doing so. Write, I pray you, a few words of consolation for your most attached friends.

---

* This is the person who received John Huss into her house at Constance.

LETTER XXIV.*

JOHN HUSS'S REPLY.†

May the God of mercy preserve and strengthen you in his grace; and may he impart to you, as well as to me, constancy in this city; for if we continue constant, we shall obtain the succour of the Lord. It is now that I learn to understand the saying of the Psalmist: Pray and meditate on the sufferings of Christ and the martyrs: for Isaiah has declared, that experience gives intelligence,

---

* This letter has been, I own, classed under the same title and the same figure as the preceding one in the collection of John Huss's Works.

† Huss commenced this letter by the following verses, which he wrote with his own hand, to console himself, and wile away the time; they are, however, so filled with *jeux de mots* and abbreviations, that it is impossible to translate them satisfactorily. We therefore give them in the original.—

Litera gavisus, respondeo capiti istud,

Cœtus, lacus, ignis, ac testis restituere

Jonam, Danielem, tres Pu...Susannam, quia fuere

Justus, castus, puri, hæc conti...Spem retinentes

In Domino justo, qui liberat in se sperantes.

Poterit qui aucam, Dominus pie, carcere tetro

Eripere clausam, quæ se fœdaverit retro,

Quam purgat carcer, donat et instruit flere,

In lachrymas risus vertens, ut nunc sciat vere

Opprobria Christi, blasphemias, lumine recto

Cernere injurias et capite Sathanæ secto

Vincere morte, vel ut sibi dederit optima vita.

and unless a man has undergone temptation, he can know nothing.

I do not understand what the Doctor of Bibrach inquires about; and I form no conjectures relative to his being negligent in writing. I only wish that he may be in good health; but that the health of the soul may be first fortified in him by the Lord. What I desire most ardently for him, is the improvement of his soul's health as well as that of his body, and after this life, eternal happiness with the saints.*

Rejoice all you who are united in the Lord; salute each other, and prepare yourselves to partake worthily of the body of the Lord before the Feast of Easter. I have not been able to participate in this holy sacrament for a length of time; and I shall still be deprived of it as long as it shall be the good pleasure of the Lord. It was the same with the apostles of Christ and a great number of the saints, who were debarred from the sacrament in prison and in desert places.

I rejoice that you are together, and that Zelizna Brada is with you in good health. I also am well, being, as I hope, in Jesus Christ; and I shall be still better after

---

* Huss here adds the following verses:—

 Nocturnus, gradus, litaniæ, singulæ horæ,
 Carceri sunt breves, vigiliæ dicere, leves.
 Passo Christo patimur: sed hæc est passio nostra,
 Nulla, vel modica, quæ tolleret crimina nostra,
 Adjuvet vos Christus, ne glutiat nunc Antichristus.

death, if I observe faithfully God's commandments. Oh!
that God would accord me sufficient time to reply to the
Chancellor of Paris, who so rashly and unjustly, and in
presence of so great an assembly, did not blush to accuse
his fellow-creature of errors! But God, perhaps, by my
death, or by his, will render all writing on my part useless, and in his last judgment will clear up every thing,
far better than I could do by any work of mine.

LETTER XXV.*

TO THE SAME.

[He again requests that the noblemen who have been his pro-
tectors should obtain him a hearing; and he prays earnestly
to have the Emperor and the Council applied to on the subject.]

Beloved friend in Christ, endeavour once more to persuade all our noblemen to solicit the Emperor and the
Council, that what they promised may take place; for
they declared to me,—" The facts alleged against you
shall be put down briefly in writing, and in an approaching

* *Hist. et Monum. Johann. Huss*, Epist. xxxv.

audience you shall reply." Our noblemen, by reminding the Emperor and the Council of their own words, can constrain them to do what they have promised. Then in the Council, with the assistance of God, will I loudly proclaim the truth; for, rather than to be thus basely stifled by them, I prefer to have my body burned with fire; but I am anxious that every Christian shall know what are my last words. I, therefore, in the name of the Most High, conjure my noble friends to act with energy, and to give me a last proof of their firmness. My trust in the Lord, noble John, my generous and most faithful friend, is unchangeable. May God award you a fitting recompense for all your kindness. I conjure you not to withdraw until all has been consummated. Oh! why am I not led forth to the funeral pile, rather than be thus prevented from being heard! I still hope that the Almighty God will deliver me from their hands through the merits of the saints. Let me know, I pray you, if I shall to-morrow be heard before the Council. Salute, from me, all my friends in Bohemia, and beseech them to pray to God for me. Should I remain in prison, it will be a great consolation to me, during my melancholy expectation of death, to know that you have exhorted the masters to remain steadfast in the truth, as well as the young maiden Petra and all her family. Recommend Master Jessenitz to take unto himself a wife. Pray my good friend Guzikon and the curé not to be angry with me for not having paid what I owed them, for it was totally out of my power. Let those persons who have aided me with their money, salute my friends in Christ of both sexes, and let them pray to God for me. No one will repay them, as well as our Lord Jesus Christ, the money they had advanced to me, it having been done for his service. I should, however, be well pleased that the richer persons paid the poorer; but I fear that in some this saying may be confirmed,—*Tzosoczy to Smyssli.**

LETTER XXVI.†

JOHN OF CHLUM TO JOHN HUSS.

[He informs him in what terms the Emperor explained, before the deputies of the Council, his views relative to the audience. He afterwards gives him some intelligence of the position and health of his friends.]

Dearest friend,—Learn that the Emperor held a conference to-day with the deputies of all the nations of the Council relative to your affairs, and in particular concerning the public audience. All at last replied to him

* Luther has not translated these words.
† *Hist. et Monum. Johann. Huss*, Epist. xlvii.

F

that he had certainly promised you a hearing; and your friends insisted on your being placed in an airy and wholesome place, that you may collect your strength and allow your mind to become tranquil, in order that, by a short respite, you may be better able to reply.

Therefore, in the name of God, quit not the truth in the slightest degree, through any dread of losing this miserable life; for it is for your greatest good that God has visited you with this trial.

Your friends in Prague are in good health, and particularly the Lord Schopeck, who rejoices exceedingly that you are shortly about to sustain the desired combat for the truth. We pray you earnestly to consign to paper your final opinion relative to the communion of the cup, and your reasons therefor, in order that it may be communicated to our friends in proper season; for there exists some difference of opinion on the subject amongst the brethren, and many are troubled thereby. They refer the matter to you and to your writings.

Your friends grieve at the reply of your jailor, and particularly Jessewitz; but the past cannot be recalled. They praise amongst themselves, and admire greatly, your firmness.

LETTER XXVII.*

TO JOHN OF CHLUM.†

[John Huss replies separately to all the articles. He also enumerates the annoyances to which he is subjected by several
bishops relative to a quantity of gold pieces which they affirm
to be in his possession.]

As well as I can remember, I know nothing more, and
I am ignorant for what object the public hearing will be
given me. I have protested in writing in presence of
notaries ; I have also addressed to the whole Council a
petition which I shewed to the patriarch, and in which I
demand to have permission accorded me to reply separately to each article, as I had already replied by writing.
The public audience will perhaps be allowed me for the
purpose of replying in a scholastic form, or perhaps
God will graciously permit me to preach.

I hope that, by the grace of God, I shall never depart,
even slightly, from the truth, such as I know it. Pray to
Him, therefore, to protect me !

As to what touches the communion of the cup, you

* *Hist. et Monum. Johann. Huss*, Epist. xlviii.

† This letter appears as if it were a reply to the preceding one, from
what is said in it about the sacrament of the cup.

possess the writing in which I have advanced my opinion
on the subject, and my reasons for holding it.   I have
nothing farther to say, except that the Scriptures and the
Epistles of Paul prescribe this practice, and that it was
in use in the primitive Church.   If possible, obtain permission for those who are anxious to partake of it from
religious motives, to do so;* but be guided in your conduct therein by circumstances.

Let my friends not conceive any alarm at my replies
in private.   I cannot see how these things could have been
otherwise, since all was decided by the Council, even previously to my being thrown into prison.   In a document
published by the Commissioners, and which has been read
to me, I am called a heresiarch, and a seducer of the people.   But I hope that what I have uttered in the shade,
will be, at a later period, preached in the open day.†

I was interrogated, the evening of the day on which I
saw John Barbat, respecting the forty-seven articles ; and
I replied as I had done in my preceding protest.   Taking
each article separately, they asked me if I desired to defend it :   my reply was, that I referred the matter to the
decision of the Council, as I had previously done, and I
asserted of each article, as previously, " It is true ; but

---

* *Si potest fieri, attentetis ut saltem permittatur per bullam illis dari,
qui ex devotione postulaverint.* It is not easy to say what Huss meant by
the expression *per bullam.*

† Sed spero quod quæ dixi sub tecto prædicabuntur super a tectu.

in such and such a sense." "Will you defend it?" they asked me; and my answer was, "No; I abide by the decision of the Council."

I call God to witness, that, under the circumstances, I saw nothing better to reply, as I had antecedently given it under my own hand that I should not defend any thing obstinately, but that I was ready to be instructed. These questions were put to me, because it was reported that I had informed the Emperor that I wished to defend three or four articles. They even asked me what I had declared to the Emperor, and I replied, that I had not said anything of the nature attributed to me.* Michael Causis was present, with a paper in his hand, and urging on the patriarch to force me to reply to his questions; and whilst this was going on, some bishops entered. Michael has invented something new. God has been pleased to allow him and Paletz to stand against me for my sins. The former scrutinises my letters and my writings; and Paletz brings forward all the conversations that we held together in bygone years.

The patriarch maintained openly that I was exceedingly rich; and an archbishop said to me, "You have seventy thousand florins." Michael asked me before them all, "Eh! what has become of that robe-full of florins? How much money of yours have the barons of Bohemia in

* John Huss adds, *Sed sicut scitis, &c.*, " but as you know," &c., and does not terminate the sentence.

safe keeping ?" Oh! certainly I suffered much to-day. One bishop said to me, " You have established a new law :" another, " You have preached all these articles ;". and I replied warmly and strongly, with the aid of God, and concluded by asking, " Why do you overwhelm me with insults ?"

Write nothing to me of the witnesses cited to appear, for no step has been taken about them, either by themselves, or by the king, or by the citizens of Prague.

LETTER XXVIII.*

[Huss replies to Peter the notary, who had encouraged him to give proofs of constancy.

This letter, says Luther, is a noble testimony in support of the saying of the Apostle Paul, that virtue will improve in affliction, and God brings forth fruits in us by temptation.]

May salvation come to thee from Jesus Christ! I dare not rashly say, with St Peter, since my fervour and courage are infinitely inferior to his, that " though all men shall be offended because of Christ, yet will I never be offended."

Jesus Christ has never, in express terms, declared me to be blessed like Peter, and has not promised me such

* *Hist. et Monum. Johann. Huss*, Epist. xxix.

precious gifts. I maintain, at the same time, against several together, an attack more vigorous in its nature and more terrible. I, however, can declare, that, having placed my trust in Jesus Christ, I shall adhere to the truth, even unto death, with the aid of the saints and his own.

If the Lord John of Chlum suffers any loss on my account, do thou, my dear Peter, take thought to repair it when thou shalt have returned. Pay attention to the master of the mint, and his wife, who imprudently engaged themselves for me, and to all our other friends, known to the Curé, my disciple. If any horse remains still my property, it ought to come into the possession of Lord John, with the car.

As to thee, if Master Martin or Master Christian live, thou shalt receive from them a part of the sixty-four or seventy pieces of money; and I wish that this portion were larger. Bear in mind, however, that I do not pretend, by this money, to recompense thy ardent and unchangeable love for the truth, or the services that thou hast rendered me, and the consolations which thou hast lavished on me in my hours of difficulty. May God be thy great recompense for all these things, for I possess nothing that is worthy of thy acceptance. Should it be granted me to live at Prague; and if my return to that city is not impossible, I would share every thing with thee like a brother. I do not, however, form any wish to return thither, but inasmuch as it may be in accordance with the will of the Lord in heaven. I do not know to whom I can entrust the viatica which I still possess, and which I had bequeathed to Master Martin. Dispose of my books according to the directions that I sent to him, and choose for thyself from amongst them such of those written by Wycliffe as shall please thee. I am much alarmed for our brethren, who, I fear, will be persecuted, unless the Lord interpose in their favour; and I am apprehensive that many will be offended.

Salute, I pray thee, with a great affection, the Bohemian and Polish noblemen, and render thanks, in particular, to the Lords Wenceslaus de Duba and John de Chlum, who, I hope, will be present at the audience of the Council.

Farewell in Jesus Christ !

LETTER XXIX.*

TO ONE OF HIS FRIENDS.

[He mentions what happened to him in the audience, which was accorded him four days before the eclipse of the sun.†]

The Lord, to-day, gave me a firm and intrepid heart. Two articles were struck out, and I am in hope that a greater number will be treated in like manner. They were all crying out, like the Jews against Jesus. They have not yet come to the principal count, viz., to the avowal that all the incriminated articles are found in my writings. You committed an error in judgment in presenting the treatise against an unknown adversary. Do not shew, with the treatise on the Church, anything besides that against Stanislaus and Paletz.

It is well that they had desired my book to be given back to them; for some persons cried out loudly to have it burned, particularly Michael de Causis, whom I myself heard. I never thought that I had, in that multitude of priests, only the brother, and a Polish doctor whom I

* *Hist. et Monum. Johann. Huss,* Epist. xxxvi.

† This is an error of Luther's; the first audience was given the day before the eclipse, on June 6.

F 2

knew to be such. I rendered thanks to the Bishop Ly-temissel, for he said but these few words : " *Atzo Huss to bie utzmil.*" *

I am grateful to you for the manner in which you have arranged the articles : it will be well to have them published under that form. The presidents have asserted that I elsewhere published another definition of the Church, and they wanted to know what it was.

Greet the lords who are believers, and the friends of the truth, and pray to God in my behalf, for I have need of it. I think they will not pardon me the opinion which I quoted from St Augustin respecting the Church, the predestinated members, the elect, and the bad bishops.

Oh! that an audience may be accorded me, in order that I may reply to the arguments by which they attack the articles of my treatises ; many of them, now crying out, would then be silent : but the will of God be done !

* The meaning of this does not appear.

LETTER XXX.*

TO HIS NOBLE BENEFACTORS.

[This letter teaches us in what consists the trial of spiritual combats; it shews how true is what we confess in the Creed, that there is but one holy and universal Church,† and that the riches of this Church are common to all. Man is for his fellow-creature, an angel and a God in misfortunes.]

I am delighted that the treatise against an unknown person has not been discovered, as well as several others.

I have been able these latter days to nourish my soul with better things,‡ than since Easter day until last Sunday. I imagined this Council to contain more order and decency. May the noble John, my friend, be blessed in eternity. I should with pleasure learn in what state is Barbat, who refused to follow the counsels of his friends.

Since they are in possession of my book, I have not felt any want of the work. Preserve carefully the list of the first articles, with the proofs; and if you should

---

* *Hist. et. Monum. Johann. Huss,* Epist. **xxxvii.**

† Catholicism.

‡ *De bonis plus comedi.* I did not think it possible to understand these words but in a figurative manner.

want any testimonies for any of the articles, assign witnesses.   The most important article is that entitled *All
that a virtuous man does, he does virtuously.*

I am suffering from a toothach, and during the heat
have been seized with vomitings of blood.   I suffered
also from the stone and headach.   These are punish-
ments for my sins, and signs of God's love.   Since they
have condemned my treatises, I pray you to suppress
the last letter written in Bohemian, which I sent to-day,
in order that the people of God should not believe that
all my books are condemned, as I was afraid of, from a
letter I received yesterday.

It would be desirable that no letter written in this
prison should be known; for what God intends to do
with me is still very uncertain.   I fear that Ulric may
have published some of my letters.   I conjure you,
therefore, in God's name, to pay the greatest attention
to the letters—to your words and acts.   Oh! how much
I was consoled by receiving your letters, and in writing
you mine!   I hope, with the grace of God, that men
may one day derive instruction from them.·

As long as I know you remain with the young-
Seigniors at Constance, I shall be comforted, even though
I should be already condemned to death.   I regard it as
certain that God has bestowed you on me, as angels to
strengthen and console me,—me, a weak and unfortunate
man, in the midst of my temptations.   What they have

been, what they are, and will still be, the Almighty God knows. He who has compassion on me, He who is my refuge, my support, and my deliverer, in Him have I placed my trust.

Two delegates of the Council asked me in prison, " If I possessed several books which I had made use of in my researches?" I answered, that " I possessed them." They asked me, " Where?" " In Bohemia," I replied. They inquired of me, " Whether I had none here?" I denied having any, which is the fact, although I had previously brought with me the book of Sentences, the Bible, and some other works. I learned from them that John, my pupil, had withdrawn; and they said to me, " Have you no other observations to offer?" " No; what I have said, is the truth." " Will you abjure and recant?" " No," I replied; " but come to the Council; there you shall hear me. I am to appear before it, and there will I answer. Why do you tempt me? Have you come to console a prisoner, or add to his affliction?" Then, after having again exchanged some words, they withdrew. Take care of the books, if you have any; as for me, I am not aware of any.

Tell Master Jessenitz, that the notary has perfidiously changed my evidence concerning the explanation of the bull, which, as you have heard, I strongly affirmed before the Council.

, .

LETTER XXXI.*

[John Huss relates with what horror and rage he was greeted by the Council.]

I, Master John Huss, in hope, servant of Christ, and ardently desiring that believers in Christ may not, when I shall have ceased to live, find in my death an opportunity for scandal, and look on me as an obstinate heretic, do take to witness Jesus Christ, for the sake of whose word I have wished to die; and I leave in writing the remembrance of these things for the friends of truth.

I had often declared, both in private, in public, and before the Council, that I would consent to an inquiry, and would submit myself to instruction, abjuration, and punishment, if it was demonstrated to me that I had written, taught, or disseminated, any thing contrary to the truth.   But fifty doctors, who stated that they were deputed by the Council, having been frequently corrected by me, and even in public, for having falsely extracted articles from my works, refused me any private explanation, and declared that they would not confer with me, saying *You ought to submit yourself to the decision of the Coun-*

---

* *Hist. et Monum. Johann. Huss*, Epist. xv.

cil. And the Council mocked when, in the public audience, I quoted the words of Christ and the holy doctors;
at one time they reproached me with misunderstanding
them, and, at another, the doctors insulted me.* . . . .

An English doctor, who had already said to me in private, that Wycliffe had wished to annihilate all science,
and had filled his books and his logic with errors, began
to discourse on the multiplication of the body of Christ
in the consecrated host, and, as his arguments were weak,
he was told to be silent; then he cried out: " This man
deceives the Council; take care that the Council be not
led into error as it was by Berenger." When he was
silent, another discussed noisily concerning the created
and common essence. All began to clamour against him.
I then demanded that he might be heard, and said to
him, " You argue well; I will answer you most willingly."
He also broke down, and he added in a sullen voice:
" *This man is a heretic.*" The Seignior Wenceslaus Duba,

---

* John Huss alludes here to a discussion, not very intelligible, on
the community of the essence in the Divine Persons. We give it in the
original: Quidam autem cardinalis supremus concilii, et a concilio de-
putatus in publica audientia, accepta una charta, dixit: Ecce unus
magister sacræ theologiæ præsentavit mihi argumentum istud, dicatis
ad illud: Erat autem argumentum de essentia communi, quam con-
cessi esse in divinis. Postea ipso deficiente, quamvis reputaretur doctor theologiæ valentissimus, dixi sibi de essentia communi creata, quæ
est primum esse creatum communicatum singulis creaturis: ex qua
ipso volebat probare remanentiam panis materialis, sed notabiliter ad
metam nescientiæ argumenti reductus obmutuit.

John de Chlum, and Peter the notary, valiant champions and friends of the truth, know what clamours, what unworthy raillery and blasphemies were poured upon me in this assembly. Stunned by so much noise, I said, " I thought there was to be found in this Council more decency, more piety, and more discipline." All then began to listen, for the Emperor had commanded silence to be observed.

The cardinal who presided said to me—" You spoke more humbly in your prison." I answered—" It is true ; for then no one clamoured against me, and now they are all vociferous." He added—" Will you submit to an investigation ?" " I consent to it," replied I, " within the limits which I have fixed." " Take this for the result of the inquiry," resumed the cardinal, " that the doctors have declared the articles extracted from your books to be errors, which you ought to efface, in abjuring those already testified against you by witnesses." The Emperor afterwards said—" This will soon be committed to writing for you, and you will answer it." " Let that be done at the next audience," said the cardinal; and the sitting closed. God knows how many trials I have suffered since !*

* For the detailed account of this second audience, consult *The Reformers before the Reformation*, vol. ii. book iv. chap. 4.

LETTER XXXII.*

TO HIS FRIENDS.

[He complains that the Emperor Sigismond had treated him with less prudence than Pontius Pilate did Jesus Christ.]

Salutation in Jesus Christ. What I am informed by Peter affords me pleasure. I do not keep his letters, but destroy them immediately. Let not the sexterni† be sent me; for I fear the danger that might accrue to the messenger and some other persons, I still earnestly entreat that all our Seigniors may solicit collectively for me a last audience with the Emperor; for, since he told me at the Council, that an audience would shortly be granted me, in order that I might reply briefly in writing, it will be a shame for him should he violate the promise which he has given me. But I believe his word on this subject will be as stable and firm as in the safe-conduct.

Several persons warned me in Bohemia not to rely on his safe-conduct; others told me that Sigismond would deliver me up to my enemies; the Seignior Mykest

---

* *Hist. et Monum. Johann. Huss*, Epist. xxxiv.
† Sexterni, a coin of these times.

was one of these.   Duvoki said to me, in the presence
of Jessenitz, " Master, regard it as a certainty that you
will be condemned." I presume that he was aware of the
Emperor's intentions. I thought the latter was well
versed in the law of God and the truth. I understand
now that his wisdom is not great. He has condemned
me before my enemies. Why has he not done like
Pilate, who, after having heard the accusers, exclaimed
—*I find nothing to condemn in this man.* If, at least,
he had said—" I have given him a safe-conduct. If he
will not submit to the Council I will send him to the king
of Bohemia, with your sentence and the testimonies in
support of it, in order that he may be judged by this
prince and his clergy." Sigismond, in fact, intimated to
me by Leffl, and others, of his intention to grant me an
audience whenever it might be necessary, and of his resolution to save me from all danger, should I not submit
to the judgment.

LETTER XXXIII.*

TO HIS FRIENDS.

[He relates the frightful visions which diversely affected him, although events have confirmed the truth of all his dreams.]

The Lord be with you ! The warning of the Lord is more precious to me than gold and topaz. I hope, then, in the mercy of Jesus Christ, that he will grant me his Spirit, that I may hold fast in the truth. Pray to the Lord ; for the spirit is willing and the flesh is weak. May the Almighty God be the reward of my well-beloved Nobles, who with a constant, fervent, and faithful heart, persevere in justice. God will enable them to know the truth in the kingdom of Bohemia. But that they may cling to it, it is necessary they return to Bohemia, forgetting vainglory in order to attach themselves to a King who is neither mortal nor subject to our miseries, but who is the King of Glory, giving eternal life.

Oh ! with what sweet pleasure did I press the hand of the Seignior John, who did not blush to offer it to me,

* *Hist. et Monum. Johann. Huss*, Epist. xxxiii.

an unfortunate man——to me, a heretic, in chains, despised and loudly condemned by all. I shall not much longer hold discourse with you; salute, therefore, our faithful Bohemians.

Paletz came to visit me in prison, and accosted me in my deep distress, by telling me, in presence of the Commissioners, that since the birth of Christ, there had risen no heretic more dangerous than Wycliffe and myself. He further declared, that all those who have listened to my preachings are infected with this heresy, which consists in affirming that the material bread remains in the sacrament of the altar. "O Paletz," I answered, "how cruel are these words! and how much thou sinnest against me. I am about to die; perhaps when I rise from my bed I shall be conducted to the stake. What reward will they give thee in Bohemia?" I should have perhaps abstained from writing these things, for fear of appearing to hate them.

I have ever kept in mind these words, "Put not your trust in princes;" and this other text, which says, "Cursed is he who trusts in man only."

Be prudent, for the sake of God, whether you should remain in this place, or whether you return; do not carry about you any of my letters, but disperse my writings amongst all our friends.

Learn that I have had a great combat to sustain, in not wondering at my dreams. I dreamed of the Pope's evasion before it took place, and after the event being related, I heard, in the night-time, the Seignior John say, " The Pope will return to you." I have dreamed of Master Jerome's captivity, but not in what way it should occur; and likewise of the different prisons to which I should be conducted, such as they were afterwards assigned to me, but without any particular details. . . . . A multitude of serpents often presented themselves before me, rolled up into a circle, the head forming the tail. I have seen many other things besides.

I write this, not that I consider myself a prophet, or that I should exalt myself, but in order to tell you I have experienced both mental and bodily temptations, as well as great fear of transgressing the precepts of our Lord Jesus Christ. I think now of these words of Jerome, who said to me, " If I go to Constance, I do not believe I shall return thence." A worthy shoemaker, André Polonus, said, whilst bidding me farewell, " May God be with you : I can hardly hope that you will return safe and sound, very dear Master John, you who cling with so much force to truth. May the King, not he of Hungary,* but of Heaven, bestow on you his blessings for the true and excellent doctrines I have learned from you."

* The Emperor Sigismund.

LETTER XXXIV.

\

May God be with you, noble Henry! I received your letter on the Wednesday before the fete of Saint Vitus, and it caused a great joy, although in prison, and in the expectation of death. I conjure you, my dear lord, to live according to God's law, keeping in your soul those things which you have heard and learned of me. If, nevertheless, some of them appear to you unworthy of being preserved, reject them. I hope, however, I have taught you nothing concerning our Lord which was against the law of God. I could write at great length on this subject; but I will say in few words, " Keep the commandments of God, be merciful unto the poor, shun pride; bear in mind these words, ' Remember what thou art, what thou wert, and what thou shalt be. . . .' " Beloved lord, keep me also in remembrance; salute for me your noble wife, your family, and all my friends; for I presume, that before my death, which is hastening on, you will never see me more; and this death I am ready for.

Written on the fifth day before the festival of Saint Vitus.

May God be with you, my dear Bohemians, and with me! for I am suffering for his Word.

LETTER XXXV.*

TO A FRIEND.

[Huss alludes to the hymn noted down on parchment, which he composed in Bohemian for Schopeck.]

You will forward the letter on parchment to the Seignior Henry Schopeck; I have kept it in my prison in remembrance of him; and I composed this hymn during my leisure hours.

Noble Henry, my faithful friend, remember the words you have heard from me, in order that you may obtain eternal glory. Remember what I have said unto you :— I am confident God will grant me his Spirit, that I may be enabled to support some temptations, for his name's sake.

Written, the Sunday before Saint Vitus, in the expectation of death.

* *Hist. et Monum. Johann. Huss*, Epist. xlii.

LETTER XXXVI.*

TO THE FAITHFUL OF BOHEMIA.

[John Huss wrote this letter in his own handwriting in his prison
  at Constance, to console the king and kingdom of Bohemia,
  and to warn them not to abandon the true Evangelical doctrine,
  nor the Chapel of Bethlehem, nor the faithful doctors of the
  Gospel, notwithstanding the rage of Satan and of the world,
  but to live in piety and justice, each one according to his
  calling.]

I, John Huss, in hope servant of God, desire, that the
believers in Bohemia who love the Lord, may live and
die in grace, and at last obtain eternal life.

You who are high in dignity, you who are rich, and
you who are poor, you all who are the faithful and well
beloved disciples of the Lord, I conjure you all to obey
God, to glorify his word, and to elevate yourselves by
listening to his precepts.   I conjure you to cling to the
divine word, which I have preached according to the law
and after the testimony of the saints ; I conjure you, if
any amongst you, either in public meetings or in private
conversations, have heard any words from me, or read
any writings of mine contrary to God's truth, not to at-

---

* *Hist. et Monum. Johann. Huss,* Epist. xi.

tach yourselves to such, although my conscience does not reproach me with having said or written any thing of the nature to which I refer. I conjure you besides, if any one has remarked any thing trifling, either in my discourses or my writings, not to imitate me in that, but to pray to God that he may pardon my frivolity; I conjure you to love priests of good morals, and to honour, in preference, those who exert themselves in diffusing the word of God; I conjure you to beware of deceitful men, especially impious priests, of whom the Lord has said, they are outwardly dressed in sheep's clothing, while within they are ravening wolves; I conjure the powerful to treat their poor servants with kindness, and to command them with justice; I conjure citizens to keep a good conscience in their profession, artizans to apply themselves carefully to their callings, and to keep before their eyes the fear of God, and domestics faithfully to serve their masters; I conjure the masters of arts to live honestly, to instruct their pupils faithfully; first of all, teaching them to fear God, afterwards exerting themselves for the glory of God, the good of their country, and their own salvation, and not to attach themselves strongly to mere rules of propriety, whether for the sake of riches or for worldly honours; I conjure the pupils of the public school, and all scholars, to obey their masters in all lawful things, and to labour with the greatest zeal, in order to advance one day the kingdom of God, their own salvation, and that of

other men. I conjure you all to bestow your thanks on
the generous noblemen, Wenceslaus Duba, John of Chlum,
Henry Plumlovic, Wylem Zagee, Nicholas, and the other
Bohemian, Moravian, and Polish Seigniors, who, as zealous defenders of God's truth, opposed this Council with
all their power, endeavouring to obtain my deliverance;
in particular, I mention Wenceslaus Duba and John of
Chlum. Believe all they may report to you, for they
were present at the Council on the days when I replied.
They know what Bohemians have risen against me; they
are acquainted with the unworthy deeds which were imputed to me by them; they are aware how the whole
assembly vociferated against me whilst I was answering
all the questions that were asked. I conjure you to pray
for the King of the Romans, and for your own, and for
the Queen, in order that the God of mercy may dwell
with them and with you, now and for ever.

I write you this letter in my prison and with my fet-
tered hand, expecting after to-morrow my sentence of
death, and having an entire confidence in God that he will
not forsake me; that he will not suffer me to renounce
his word, or abjure errors wickedly ascribed to me by
false witnesses. When we shall meet again in a happy
eternity you will know with what clemency the Lord
deigns to assist me in my cruel trials.

I know nothing concerning Jerome, my faithful friend,
unless that he is detained in a wretched prison, waiting,

like myself, for death, on account of that faith which he so courageously spread through Bohemia. But the Bohemians, our most cruel adversaries, have delivered us to the power of other enemies and to their chains. Pray to God for them. I conjure you, inhabitants of Prague, above all to love my Chapel of Bethlehem, and to have the word of God preached there, should God permit it. The fury of Satan is stirred up against that place. Seeing that the power of darkness was weakened in it, he has excited the parochial clergy against that temple. I hope God will protect it, and that his word will be preached there with more success by others than by me, a weak and infirm man. Lastly, I conjure you to love one another, to shut out no one from the path of divine truth, and to watch that the upright be not oppressed by violence. Amen.

Written on the night of the Monday before Saint Vitus, and sent by a good and faithful German.

LETTER XXXVII.*

(NOT ADDRESSED TO ANY BODY.)

[The authentic profession of faith, in which John Huss declares,
with the assistance of our Lord Jesus Christ, that he will not
abjure the truth which he has acknowledged, unless further enlightened by the Scriptures.]

My last and firm determination is, that I refuse to
confess as erroneous the articles which have been truly
extracted from my works, and that I refuse to abjure
those which have been attributed to me by false witnesses; for to abjure implies that one has held erroneous opinions—it is, in fact, to reject them, and adopt
others of a contrary tendency. God knows that I have
never taught these errors, imputed to me by those who
have retrenched from my works many truths and falsified
them. Were I aware that, in the articles I confess to,
there was one contrary to the truth, I would correct it,
and most heartily strike it out. Nay, I would teach and
preach the contrary. But, although some parts may be
considered scandalous and erroneous by those who are
displeased with such doctrines, yet I do not believe that
there is a single passage which is opposed to the law of
Christ or to the words of the holy apostles.

* *Hist. et Monum. Johann. Huss*, Epist. xx.

I detest and condemn all false interpretation imputed to my articles against my intention, submitting myself to the correction of our Divine Master, and confiding in his infinite mercy, that he himself may deign to wash me clean from such sins as I am ignorant of.* I return thanks to all the Bohemian Barons, and especially to King Wenceslaus, and to the Queen, my gracious Sovereign, that they have loved me, have acted piously towards me, and have worked ardently to procure my deliverance; I render thanks also to the Emperor Sigismund, for his good intentions in my favour; I render thanks to all those Nobles of Bohemia and Poland who have shewn themselves firm in defending the truth, and in endeavouring to break my chains; I desire the salvation of all, here below in grace, and afterwards in a glorious eternity.

May the God of all goodness bring you back into Bohemia with perfect health of body and soul, that, serving in this world, Christ, our Sovereign, you may attain eternal life!

You will salute for me all my friends, to whom I cannot write; if I saluted by name some, and not others, I should appear to except some persons; and those to whom I did not write would think I did not keep them in remembrance, or did not love them as I ought to do.

---

* Quod ab occultis peccatis meis ipse me mundavit.

Written in prison, and in chains, the sixth day before the festival of St John the Baptist.

JOHN HUSS, in hope, servant of Christ.

LETTER XXXVIII.*

TO HIS DISCIPLE, MASTER MARTIN.

Master Martin, my dear disciple, my well-beloved brother in Christ, live according to the law of Christ ; be zealous in the preaching of God's Word. I conjure you, in the name of the Lord, not to seek rich clothing like unto that which I was fond of, alas! and which I wore, neglecting to shew an example of humility to the people whom I instructed. Attach thy soul to the reading of the Bible, and especially that of the New Testament ; and in obscure passages, have recourse to commentators as much as it is in thy power to do so.

Dread the intercourse of women, and be circumspect, when thou listenest to them at confession, lest thou shouldest be caught in the snares of unlawful desires ; for

---

* *Hist. et Monum. Johann. Huss*, Epist. xxviii.

I hope thou hast guarded all thy purity, and that thou belongest wholly to God.

Be not afraid of dying, if thou wouldest wish to live with Christ, for he has said himself, Fear not those who destroy the body, but cannot kill the soul. If they should ask thee concerning thy adherence to my doctrines, answer, "I believe my master has been a good Christian, in what he has taught and written; I have neither read all, nor understood all. I speak as I think." I hope that the mercy of God, with the aid of well-disposed people, will enable us to live in peace, although Paletz labours with his associates to get all my adherents condemned. But know that the Lord lives, who can in his grace preserve you, and can confound and destroy all the enemies of his word.

I recommend to thee my very dear brethren; act towards them as thou knowest is right. Thou wilt salute Peter, with his wife and family, and all those who belong to the Church of Bethlehem: Catherine, that holy girl, and the Curé Guzikon, Maurice Hatzer, and all the friends of the truth; Geskonière, the Seignior Gregory, all the Masters, Jessenitz, Kuba, the two Simons, and Nicholas Haulikon. Let all those who possess, or shall possess, my books be prudent. Thou wilt also salute all my well-beloved brothers in Christ, the doctors, the writers, the shoemakers, the tailors, in recommending them to be zealous for the laws of Christ, to advance humbly in wisdom, and not to make use of their own commentaries, but to have recourse to those of the saints. Thou wilt tell Henry Liffel to give to Jacob, the writer, the piece of money which was promised him.

Salute Matthew, formerly my disciple at Bethlehem, and especially Master Matthew Chudy, and the faithful John Vitlis, that they may pray for me, a sinner.

Incline my brother's sons to exercise some worldly calling; for I should be afraid, if they took upon them a spiritual charge, that they might not fill it as they should do. Satisfy as well as thou canst, those to whom I owe something; should they wish, nevertheless, to forget these debts for the love of the Lord, the Lord will bestow on them much greater riches.

Keep in mind all the good thou hast heard from my lips; and if thou hast discovered in me any thing which was not according to propriety, detest it, and pray to God that he may deign to pardon me. Meditate without ceasing on what thou art, on what thou hast been, and what thou mayest become. Deplore the past, amend the present, dread the future, that is, sin.

May the God of grace console thee, as well as all our above-mentioned brethren, that He may conduct you with all the others to his glory, in which, I firmly hope, of his mercy, all will rejoice before thirty years have passed over.

Adieu, my well-beloved brother; dwell always with

Christ Jesus, thou, and all those who love the name of our Lord.

Written in prison the Sunday after Saint Vitus.

JOHN HUSS, in hope, servant of God.

LETTER XXXIX.*

TO THE LORD HAULIKON.

[Huss invites him not to oppose administering the blood of Jesus Christ to laymen under the form of wine.]

As a preacher of the word of Christ, my very dear brother, do not oppose the administering of the Cup, it being a Sacrament instituted by Jesus Christ and his apostles. No text of Scripture is opposed to it, but only custom; and I think that this was established only through negligence and forgetfulness. But it is not custom which we should follow, but the example of Christ. The Council, alleging custom as a motive, has declared the Communion of the Cup by layman to be an error, and has ordained, that whosoever should practise it, shall

* *Hist. et. Monum. Johann. Huss,* Epist. xvi.

G 2

be punished as a heretic, if he did not amend this practice.   Already, then, has the ,malice of men condemned as an error an institution of Christ.   I conjure you, by the love of God, not to attack Master Jacobel, that there may not be any division amongst the faithful, and that Satan may not find a new subject for joy. Prepare yourself as quickly as possible, my dear brother, to suffer for the Communion of the Cup.   Lay aside all fears which is unworthy of you, and remain firm in the truth of Christ, exhorting the other brethren by the Gospel of our Lord Jesus Christ,   I think that they will give you, in support of the Communion of the Cup, what I have written at Constance.   Salute the faithful in Christ,

Written in irons, on the eve of the day of the Ten Thousand,

LETTER XL.*

TO SOME FRIENDS.

[Great victory over the gates of hell, and over those who, with unexampled cunning, and under specious pretexts, solicited John Huss to abjure the truth of the Lord.]

A multitude of people have come to exhort me, and amongst them many doctors, but few brethren, as the Apostle has said. They were prodigal in their counsels and phrases; they told me, that I could and I ought to abjure my scruples in submitting my will to the Holy Church, which the Council represents; but not one of them can avoid the difficulty, when I place him in my situation, and ask him, if, being certain of having never preached, or defended, or entertained heresy, he could, in safe conscience, formally confess that he abjured an error which he never supported. Some of them stated, that it was not necessary to abjure, but merely to renounce the heresy held or not held; others maintain, that to abjure signifies to deny what is attested rightly or erroneously. I would willingly swear, I replied to them, that I have never preached, held, or defended, the errors which are imputed

* *Hist. et Monum. Johann. Huss, Epist.* xxx.

to me; and that I will never preach, hold, or defend them. And when I spoke thus, they immediately retired.

Others insist that, supposing a man really innocent were found in the Church, and this man, through humility, confess himself guilty, he would be well deserving : thereupon some one cited, amongst the ancient fathers, a certain saint, in whose bed had been covertly put a prohibited book. Inculpated and examined on this subject, the saint denied the fault, but his enemies answered, " Thou hast concealed the book, and put it in thy bed ;" and this book having been found there, the saint confessed himself culpable. Some supported this opinion by the example of a certain holy woman, who lived in a monastery in the disguise of a man. She was accused of being the father of a child. She confessed it, and kept the child : her innocence was afterwards discovered with her sex. Many other means were also`proposed to me.

An Englishman addressed me thus, " Were I in your place, I would abjure ; for in England, all the masters, and all men held in consideration, who were suspected of adhering to the opinions of Wycliffe, have been severally cited before the archbishop, and have abjured."

Lastly, yesterday they were all agreed in engaging me to place myself at the mercy of the Council.

Paletz came at my entreaty, for I desired to confess to him. I asked the commissioners, and those who ex-

horted me, to give me for confessor either him or another.
And I said, " Paletz is my principal adversary ; I wish
to confess to him ; or, at least, give me in his stead a man
qualified to hear me : I conjure you to do so in the name
of the Lord." This last desire was accorded : I confessed
to a monk, who piously and most patiently listened to me ;
he gave me absolution, and counselled me, but did not
enjoin me, to follow the advice of others.

Paletz came : he wept with me when I besought him
to pardon me for having uttered before him some offensive
words, and especially for having called him a forger of
writings. And as I reminded him that, in a public audience, when he heard me deny the articles cited by the
witnesses, he rose up and cried : " This man does not
believe in God,"—he denied it, but truly he said it,
and perhaps you heard him do so. I reminded him, in
what manner he said to me in prison, in presence of the
Commissioners, " Since the birth of Christ, no heretic
has written more dangerously than Wycliffe and thou."
He also insisted, that all those who have read my sermons
are infected with the error concerning the sacrament of
the altar. He has now denied it, adding, " I did not
say all, but a great number." And yet it is certain that
he said it. And when I took him up by saying, " Oh!
Master Paletz, how much you wrong me in accusing my
auditory of heresy !" he did not reply anything, and he
exhorted me, like the others, always repeating, that

through me and mine much harm had been done. He told me, also, that he possessed a letter addressed to the Bohemians, in which was written, that, at the Chateau, I sang some verses on my captivity. In the name of Heaven, take great care of my letters : do not let them be carried to any clerical person, and let our Seigniors only trust some laymen. Inform me whether they accompany the Emperor. Jesus Christ, by his grace, preserves me immoveable in my first resolution.

JOHN HUSS, in hope, servant of God,

LETTER XLI.*

TO JOHN CARDINAL.

[John Huss replies to the Father, that is to say, to the Cardinal,†
clearly establishing, that it is better to die for the truth than
to depart from it, though only a nail's breadth, even under
the false pretext of the good of the Church.]

May the Almighty God, sovereignly good and wise,

---

* *Hist. et Monum. Johann. Huss*, Epist. xxxix.

† Luther erroneously believed that the person whom John Huss
only designates under the name of Father, for fear of compromising
him, was the Cardinal of Osti. J. Lenfant has clearly demonstrated
that the person, to whom John Huss gives this name, was a monk
called John Cardinal. (See the *History of the Council of Constance*,
book iii.)

The following is the form of revocation he invited John Huss to
sign, and which Luther has inserted in the collection of John Huss's
letters, under the number xxxviii.

" I, the undersigned, besides the protest which I have already made,
and do here repeat, again protest, that although many things which I
have never thought of have been imputed to me; nevertheless, for all
the things which I am accused of, whether extracted from my works,
or obtained from the deposition of witnesses, I humbly submit myself
to the mercy, judgment, explanation, and correction of the Holy Coun-

deign to bestow on my Father eternal life, for the sake of our Lord Jesus Christ!

Reverend Father, I am most grateful for your benevolent and paternal interest. I dare not submit myself to the Council in the limits that you trace out to me; whether because I should be obliged to condemn many truths that they term fraudulent; or because I should be obliged to perjure myself by abjuring and confessing that I had held errors, by which I have greatly scandalized the people of God, who have heard me say the contrary in my preaching.

If, then, in the Book of the Maccabees, it is written of Eleazar, a man of the ancient law, that he refused to lie, by confessing that he had eaten meats prohibited by the ancient law, for fear of acting thus against God, and leaving a bad example to posterity; how should I, a priest of the new law, although unworthy, through the terror of pain of a short duration, consent gravely to transgress the law of God, by keeping back from the truth, by perjuring myself, and, lastly, by offending my neighbour?

Truly, it is more advantageous to die than to fall into the hands of God by flying from a momentary evil, and perhaps afterwards to fall into the fire, and into eternal

cil General, in order to abjure, revoke, and retract them. I will submit to penance, and will do all that the Holy Council shall decide in its mercy for my salvation, throwing myself on its indulgence, and recommending myself to it with entire discretion."

2

opprobrium. Therefore, since I have appealed to Jesus Christ, to the Judge sovereignly just and powerful, confiding to him my cause, I am resolved to adhere to his decision, and to his holy and sacred sentence, knowing that he will judge all men, not according to false witnesses, or to the errors of councils, but according to the truth, and their own merits.

LETTER XLII.*

JOHN CARDINAL TO JOHN HUSS.

[The Father insists on the counsel which he has given: " whoever thou mayest be who readest these pages, see how the false title of the Church deceives the excellent Cardinal."†]

In the first place, my well-beloved brother, do not let yourself be troubled by the fear of condemning truths; for it is not you who will condemn these, but those who are your superiors and ours. Meditate on these words, " Rely not on your own prudence." There are many wise and conscientious men in the Council : " My son, listen to thy mother's law." This is my point.

* *Hist. et Monum. Johann. Huss*, Epist. xl.
† Luther falls again into the same error; see note 2 of page 159.

I come to the second, concerning the perjury of the matter. This perjury, even if it be one, will not fall on you, but on those who exact it. Heresy ceases· where obstinacy ends. Augustin, Origen, the Master of the Sentences, and many others, have erred, and returned with joy from their errors; I also often thought that I perfectly understood certain things, in which I was mistaken. When better informed, I returned with eagerness to a different opinion.

I write briefly; for I write to an intelligent man. Do not stray from the truth, but arrive at it; you will not perjure yourself but will become better. Do not offend, but edify. The Jew Eleazar obtained a great glory, but Judas with his seven sons, and the eight martyrs, obtained much greater. Paul did not hesitate to be let down in a basket in order to propagate a better law. May Jesus Christ, the Judge of your appeal, accord you apostles like these.* Some combats for the faith of Jesus Christ are still due from you.

---

* This passage is exceedingly obscure. It may be seen that it relates to what John Huss had said that he would appeal to Jesus Christ. In law are called apostles certain letters which the appellant ought to obtain from the judges to whom he has appealed; because, if they are not obtained after a certain delay, he is supposed to have renounced his appeal, and is obliged to submit to his first judgment.— Lenfant, *History of the Council of Constance.*

LETTER XLIII.*

[Huss relates another'combat of the flesh and spirit for the confession of the truth, a combat worthy of fixing the attention of
pious men.]

Salutation to you, through Jesus Christ! I beseech
you, for God's sake, not to shew my letters, nor to publish them; for I fear they might place several persons in
jeopardy. If Vitus remains, let him be prudent. I rejoice greatly to learn that my gracious Lord is coming to
me. Our Saviour raised up Lazarus to life on the fourth
day, when he already began to decay. He preserved
Jonas in the belly of the fish, and restored him to his
preaching; he drew Daniel in safety from the lion's den
that he might write his prophecies; he preserved from
the flames the three young men in the furnace; and he
delivered Susannah, already condemned and on the point
of perishing.

Wherefore, he could as easily snatch also from prison
and death me, unfortunate man that I am, were it conducive
to the glory and advantage of the faithful, and to my own
welfare. The power of Him who drew Peter out of prison

* *Hist. et Monum. Johann Huss*, Epist. xxxii.

by his angel, when condemned to die at Jerusalem, and who caused the chains to fall from his hands, is not diminished.   But let the Lord's will be done; may it be fully accomplished in me for his glory and my sins !

A Doctor said to me—" If in all things I would submit to the Council; every thing would then be good and legitimate for me."   He added—" If the Council asserted you had but one eye, although you have two, still it would be necessary to say the Council was right."   " If the whole world," replied I, " should affirm such a thing, I could not, as long as I possess the use of my reason, assent to it, without wounding my conscience."   After other conversation he abandoned his argument and said to me, " I confess I have not chosen my example well."

The Lord is with me like a valiant warrior; the Saviour is my light and salvation; whom should I fear? The Lord defends my life; who shall make me tremble?   In these latter times I often repeat this sentence —" Lord, I suffer violence, answer for me; for what shall I say to my enemies ?"

JOHN HUSS, servant in hope of Jesus Christ.

LETTER XLIV.*

TO A FRIEND.

[An admirable confession of the infirmities of human nature.
The latter does not struggle against evil only, for the flesh
strives perpetually against the Spirit, and is not easily brought
under its yoke.   Reader, peruse this letter, and rejoice.†]

Salutation to you, through Jesus Christ!   Learn, very
dear friend, that Paletz, in endeavouring to persuade me,
told me that I ought not to dread the shame of an abjuration, but to think only of the good which would ensue
from it.   I answered, " The opprobrium of being condemned and burned is greater than that of sincerely abjuring.   What shame should I fear, then, in abjuring?
But tell me, Paletz, how wouldest thou act if thou wert
assured that errors were falsely imputed to thee?   Wouldest
thou wish to abjure them?"   " That, in fact, would be
hard," replied he; and he wept.   We afterwards spoke
of many things which I refuted.

Michael de Causis, this miserable man, has appeared
several times before my prison with the deputies of the
Council, and whilst I was with them, said to the keepers,

---

* *Hist. et Monum. Johann. Huss,* Epist. xxx.

† We remind the reader that the headings of the ·Letters being
written by Luther, we have not in any way changed them.

"*By the grace of God, we shall soon burn this heretic, on whom I have spent many florins.*" Know, my friend, that nevertheless I do not express in this letter a vow of vengeance : I leave it to God, and I pray for this man from the bottom of my heart.

I again exhort you to be prudent with my letters. Michael has forbidden that any person should be introduced into my prison, even the wives of my keepers. O Great God! how far does Antichrist extend his power and cruelty! but I trust that his reign will be cut short, and his iniquity laid bare, in the midst of a faithful people.

The Almighty God will strengthen the hearts of the faithful whom he has destined, from before the beginning of the world, to the crown of immortal glory. Though Antichrist shall exercise his fury as he pleases, nevertheless he shall not be able to prevail against Christ, who, according to the words of the Apostle, will destroy him by a single breath of his mouth; and the creature then shall be delivered from the bondage of corruption, and clothe itself, says the Apostle, with the glorious liberty of the sons of God! .   .   .   .

I am greatly consoled by these words of our Saviour, " Blessed are ye when men shall hate you, and when they shall separate you from their company, and shall reproach you, and cast out your name as evil, for the Son of Man's sake. Rejoice ye in that day, and leap for joy; for, behold, your reward is great in heaven." (Luke vi.) An admirable consolation, though difficult, not to understand, but to receive well ; for it invites us to delight in afflictions.

Saint James observed this rule, with the other Apostles. " Count it," says he, " all joy when ye fall into divers temptations, knowing this, that the trying of your faith worketh patience ; but let patience have her perfect work." (St James, chap. i.)   Truly it is difficult to rejoice thus with an unshaken heart, and to consider all trials as subjects for rejoicing : it is easy to say, but difficult to do it.   He who was the most patient and the most intrepid, who knew that he should rise again the third day, should vanquish his enemies by his death, and redeem his elect from condemnation, was, nevertheless, troubled in mind after the Last Supper, and cried, " My soul is exceeding sorrowful unto death."   The Gospel informs us that he groaned and trembled ; that an angel comforted him in his agony ; and that his sweat was, as it were, great drops of blood falling down to the ground. But, in his agony, he said to his disciples : " Let not your heart be troubled ; for I shall be with you to the end of the world."

And his valiant soldiers, their eyes fixed upon their Chief, the King of Glory, have endured a great combat. They have passed through fire and water, and have not perished ; and have received from the Lord that crown, alluded to by St James, when he says, " Blessed is the man that endureth temptation : for when he is tried, he shall receive the crown of life, which the Lord has promised to them that love him." A glorious crown! which the Saviour will grant to me, I firmly hope, and to you also, fervent defenders of the truth, and to all those who persevere in the love of our Saviour Jesus Christ, who has suffered for us, bequeathing us his example, that we might follow in his footsteps. It was necessary that he should suffer, as he himself has declared ; and we, who are his members, must suffer with Him who is our Head ; for he has said : " If any one will come with me, let him take up his cross and follow me ! "

O Divine Jesus, draw us nigh unto thee, weak as we are ; for, if thou dost not draw us nigh unto thee, we cannot follow thee. Fortify my spirit, that it may become strong and resolute. The flesh is weak ; but let thy grace protect, assist, and save us ; for without thee we can do nothing, and are, above all, incapable of facing, on thy account, a cruel death. Give me a determined mind, an intrepid heart, a pure faith, and perfect charity, that I may be enabled to lay down my life for thee, with patience and joy. Amen.

Written in prison and in irons, on the eve of the festival of St John the Baptist, who was decapitated for having risen up against the corruption of the wicked. May he pray for us to Jesus our Lord !

LETTER XLV.*

TO A FRIEND.

To-morrow, at six o'clock, I am to answer on the following points :—I am asked, in the first place, if I am willing to acknowledge as erroneous all the articles extracted from my books, if I abjure them, and if I engage to preach the contrary? In the second place, whether I am willing to confess that I have preached the articles imputed to me by witnesses? Thirdly, and lastly, if I abjure them? God grant that the Emperor may hear the words which God will put into my mouth; and if I am accorded pens and paper, as I hope I shall, by the grace of God I will make the following answers in writing :—

" I, John, servant of Jesus Christ, refuse to confess that any of the articles extracted from my books are erroneous, through fear of condemning the opinions of the holy doctors, and, above all, of St Augustin. Secondly, I refuse to admit that I have held or preached the articles which are imputed to me by false witnesses. Thirdly, I refuse to abjure, through fear of perjuring myself."

In the name of Heaven take great care of my letters,

* *Hist. et Monum. Johann. Huss*, Epist. xxvii.

H.

and send them to Bohemia with precaution, lest they may place many persons in danger. Keep me in remembrance, should you not receive news from me again; and pray to God that he may bestow constancy on me and Jerome, my brother in Christ; for I believe, as I understood from the deputies, that he will suffer death with me.

LETTER XLVI.*

TO HIS FRIENDS.

[Last resolution of John Huss, to which, with the grace of God, he desires to remain faithful.]†

*　　　*　　　*　　　*　　　*　　　*

These are the things which the Council has often required of me; but they imply that I revoke, that I abjure, and that I accept a penance; and I cannot do it, without denying, in many things, the truth. In the second place, I should perjure myself in abjuring and confessing errors falsely *imputed* to me. In the third place, I should afford a great scandal to the people of

---

* *Hist. et Monum. Johann. Huss*, Epist. xlv.

† This letter, such as it has reached us, is, without doubt, only a fragment; the first words indicate as much.

God who have listened to my sermons; and it would be better that a millstone were tied round my neck, and that I were plunged to the bottom of the sea. Lastly, If I acted in this manner, to avoid a momentary confusion and a short trial, I should fall into *disgrace* and *much more terrible sufferings*, unless, indeed, I repented of them before my death. Wherefore, in order to fortify myself, I have thought of the seven martyrs of the Maccabees, who preferred rather to be torn in pieces than partake of meats prohibited by God. I have thought of St Eleazar, who, according to what is written, was not willing to confess he had eaten of prohibited meats, for fear of leaving a bad example to posterity, but preferred martyrdom. Having, then, before my eyes many saints of the new law, who accepted martyrdom rather than consent to sin, how should I, who have exhorted others in my preachings to patience and firmness, be thus guilty of perjury, and of so many vile falsehoods, and scandalize also, by my example, many children of the Lord?

Far, far from me be such a thought! Our Saviour Jesus Christ will reward me fully, and bestow on me in my trials the assistance of patience.

TO HIS FRIENDS AT PRAGUE.

[He encourages and exhorts them not to be frightened on account
of the Council having delivered his writings to the flames.
He reminds them of the corrupted morals of that assembly,
and of the condemnation of Pope John.]

I ought to warn you, my well-beloved, not to let yourselves be alarmed by the sentence of those who have condemned my books to be burned.   Remember that the
Israelites burned the writings of the prophet Jeremiah,
without, nevertheless, being able to avoid the lot which
he predicted for them.   God even commanded, after the
destruction by fire of this prophecy, that a new and more
extended one should be written, which was done; for
Jeremiah dictated it in his prison, and Baruch wrote, as
it is written in chapter xxxvi. or xlv. of Jeremiah. It is
also written in the Book of Maccabees, that impious men
burned the law of God, and killed all those who were the
depositaries of it.   Under the new alliance they burned
the saints with the books of the divine law. The Cardinals condemned and delivered to the flames many books
of St Gregory, and would have burned them all, if they
had not been preserved by his servant Peter.   Two

* *Hist. et Monum. Johann. Huss*, Epist. xiii.

Councils of priests condemned St Chrysostom as a heretic;
but God made their lie manifest after the death of him
who was surnamed *St John of the Golden Mouth.*

Knowing, therefore, these things, let not fear prevent
you from reading my books, and do not deliver them up
to my enemies to be burned.   Remember that the Lord
has said, Before the day of judgment there shall be a
great desolation, such as has not been witnessed since the
beginning of the world to this day; and such, if it were
possible, the elect themselves might be led astray; but
on account of them these days shall be shortened. Think
of that, my well-beloved, and be firm.   This Council of
Constance will not extend to Bohemia; many of those
who compose it will die before they have succeeded in
forcing my books from you.   The majority will be dispersed on every side like storks; and they will discover,
on the approach of winter, what they shall have done in
summer.*   Consider that they have declared the Pope,
their chief, worthy of death for his enormous crimes.
Courage, and reply to these preachers who teach that the
Pope is God on earth; that he can sell the sacraments,
as the canonists declare; that he is the head of the
Church in administering it purely; that he is the heart
of the Church in vivifying it spiritually; that he is the
source whence springs all virtue and all good; that he is
the sun of the holy Church, the certain asylum, where it

* John Huss was burned to death in the month of July.

is important that all Christians should find refuge. Behold! already this head is, as it were, severed by the sword; already this terrestrial god is enchained; already his sins are laid bare; this never-failing source is dried up—this divine sun is dimmed—this heart has been torn and branded with reprobation, that no one should seek an asylum in it. The Council has condemned its chief, its own head, for having sold indulgences, bishopricks, and other things. But among those who have condemned him are to be found a great number of purchasers, who have, in their turn, engaged also in this unworthy traffic. There was amongst them the bishop, John Litomissel, who twice wished to buy the bishoprick of Prague; but others had the advantage over him. O! corrupt men! Why have they not, first of all, torn the beam from their own eyes; since it is written in their own law: " Whoever shall purchase a dignity with money shall be deprived of it." Sellers, therefore, and buyers, and whosoever shall interfere in this shameful contract, be ye condemned, as St Peter condemned Simon, who wished to buy from him the virtue of the Holy Ghost.

They have anathematized the seller and condemned him, and they themselves are the purchasers; they have affixed their hands to this pact, and they remain unpunished! What do I say? They traffic in this merchandise even in their very dwellings! There is in Constance one bishop who has bought, another who has sold, and the

Pope, for having approved of the bargain, has received money from the two parties. * * If God had said to the members of this Council, " Let him amongst you who is without sin pronounce the sentence of Pope John," undoubtedly they would have withdrawn one after the other. Why did they formerly bend their knees before him ? Why did they kiss his feet ? Why did they term him most holy, when they saw in him a homicide, a heretic, and a hardened sinner ? For in this manner did they already speak of him in public. Why did the Cardinals elect him Pope, knowing that he had caused the death of his predecessor ?* Why did they suffer him, since his accession to that office, to traffic in holy things? Do they not form his Council, to remind him of what is just ? and are they not as much to blame as he for these crimes, since they tolerated in him vices which were common to them all ? Why did no one dare resist him before his flight from Constance ? They all feared him then, as their very holy father ; but when, with the permission of God, the secular power laid hold of him, then they conspired and resolved that he should not escape death.

Truly, already have the malice, abomination, and turpitude of antichrist been revealed in the Pope and other members of this Council. The faithful servants of God may now understand these words of the Saviour,

* See the *Reformers before the Reformation*, vol. i., book i.

who has said, "When you shall behold the abomination of desolation foretold by the prophet Daniel," &c. Truly, the supreme abomination is pride, avarice, and simony in deserted places,—that is, in dignities, where neither goodness nor humility, nor any virtue, is now to be found, as we now witness in those who are high in honour and places. Oh! how much I desire to unveil all the iniquities that I am acquainted with, in order that the faithful servants of God may keep on their guard against them! But I hope that God will send after me more vigorous champions; and there are now already those who will better expose all the cunning tricks of antichrist, and who will expose themselves to death for the truth of our Lord Jesus Christ, who will give unto you and me eternal beatitude!

I write this letter on the day of St John the Baptist, in prison and in chains, and I bear in mind that St John was beheaded in prison for the word of God.

LETTER XLVIII.*

JOHN HUSS TO THE UNIVERSITY OF PRAGUE.

Honourable Masters, bachelors, and students, of the University of Prague, you whom I cherish in Christ Jesus, I exhort you all to love one another, to extirpate schism; to honour God above all things; in reminding yourselves how much I have always desired that the progress of our University should turn to the glory of God; how much I have bewailed your discords and your violence, and how I have always endeavoured to maintain united our illustrious nation. Remember also how much my life has been embittered by the outrages and blasphemies of some amongst those whom I most loved, and for whom I would willingly have exposed my life. And now they inflict on me a cruel death? May the Almighty God forgive them, for they know not what they do; and I pray with a sincere heart that he may spare them! My well beloved in Jesus Christ, dwell in the truth that you have known, which triumphs over all, and which increases in strength even unto eternity.

Know, also, that I have neither revoked nor abjured

---

* *Hist. et Monum. Johann. Huss*, Epist. xviii.

H 2

any article.   The Council wished that I should acknowledge as false and erroneous all the articles extracted
from my books.   I have refused, unless they proved to me
their falsehood by the Scriptures.   If there is really some
erroneous meaning in these articles I detest it, and refer
its correction to our Lord Jesus Christ, who knows my
sincerity, and is aware that my intention is not to maintain an error.   And all of you likewise do I exhort, in the
Lord, to detest every error that you may discover in my
works ; but in respecting that truth, which I have ever
kept in view, pray for me, and support each other in the
peace of God.

I, John Huss, in chains, and already on the verge of
the present life, awaiting to-morrow a cruel death, which,
I hope, will wash away my sins, not finding in myself any
heresy, by the grace of God, confess with all my soul the
truth in which I believe.

Written five days before the Festival of St Peter.

I conjure you to love Bethlehem, and to put Gallus in
my place ; for I think the Lord is with him.   I recommend to you Peter de Maldoniewitz, my very faithful and
courageous comforter.

LETTER XLIX.*

TO HIS FRIENDS.

[He explains to them how God permits his elect to be put to death, and cites several examples by which he sustains and consoles himself.]

My well beloved in the Lord, many causes, and especially the expectation of my speedy death, had made me suppose that the letters I recently wrote to you would be the last. Now that a delay is accorded——since it is permitted me to converse with you by letter, I write to you again, to testify, at least, all my gratitude. In what concerns my death, God only knows why it is deferred, as also that of my very dear brother Jerome, who, I hope, will die in a holy manner, and without a stain. I know that he acts and suffers now with more firmness than I, infirm sinner that I am. God has granted us much time, that we might better recall all our sins, and direct ourselves with greater energy to repentance ; he has given us this time, that a long and great trial might efface our sins, and thus bring consolation with it. He has granted it to us, that we might meditate on the execrable out-

* *Hist. et Monum. Johann. Huss*, Epist. xiv.

rages and cruel death of our King and merciful Lord, Jesus Christ, and that we should thus support our own evils
with greater constancy; that we might at last remember
that the joys of eternal life do not immediately follow this
world's joys, but that it is by passing through great tribulations that the saints enter the kingdom of God.
Some of them have been, without shrinking, sawed in
twain; others have been burned, stripped of their skin,
buried alive, stoned, crucified, crushed between millstones,
dragged here and there unto death, precipitated to the
bottom of the waters, strangled, cut into pieces, overwhelmed by outrages before their death, and tortured by
hunger in their prisons and in their chains. Who could
describe the torments and agonies which all the saints
have suffered for the divine truth under the old and new
covenant, and especially those who have branded the iniquity of priests, and who have raised their voices against
it? It would be a strange thing at present to remain
unpunished when attacking the perversity of priests, who
will not endure any blame.

I rejoice that they are now obliged to read my works,
where their corruption is depicted, and I know they read
them with greater attention than the Holy Scriptures, in
the ardent desire of finding out errors.

*Written on the Thursday before the Festival of Saint
Peter.*

LETTER L.*

TO THE SAME.

[John Huss relates how the Council, on the deposition of false witnesses, and on account of his works, has condemned him, without having read them.]

I have resolved, dear and faithful friends in our Lord, to make known to you in what manner the Council of Constance, swelled with so much pride and avarice, has condemned as heretical my books, written in the Bohemian tongue, without ever having seen or read them, and which it could not have understood, even when it had listened to the reading of them. For this Council is filled with Italians, French, Germans, Spaniards, and persons from all countries, and of every different language. They could not be understood but by Bishop John de Litomissel, by several Bohemians, my enemies, and by a few priests of Prague, who have first to calumniate the truth of God, and afterwards our Bohemia, which I hope is a country of a perfect faith, remarkable for its attachment to the Word of God, as well as for its good morals. And if you had been at Constance you would have witnessed

* *Hist. et Monum. Johann. Huss*, Epist. xii.

the detestable abomination of this Council, which calls itself infallible and very holy; an abomination of which, many of the country of the Grisons have said, the city of Constance could not wash herself of in thirty years, and almost every body, supporting with great difficulty the great corruption, which is to be seen in it, is irritated against the Council. When I first appeared in the presence of this assembly to reply to my adversaries, seeing that every thing was done without order, and hearing a general clamour, I cried aloud, " I thought the Council had possessed more good breeding, charity, and discipline." Then the first of the Cardinals answered, " Is it thus that thou speakest? Thy language was more modest in prison." " Yes," I replied, " for in prison no one vociferated against me; and now you are all vociferous." It is thus this Council, which has done more evil than good, has acted towards me with inordinate violence. O my faithful friends, my well-beloved in God, suffer not yourselves to be alarmed at the sentence these men have delivered against my books. Like insects, they will disperse here and there, and there, like winged insects, their ordinances will endure as long as the spiders' webs. They endeavoured to shake my perseverance in the Word of God, but they were not able to daunt the courage which God had armed me with. They refused to examine the Scriptures with me, although my words were supported by the testimonies of several noble Seigniors ready to suffer ignominy with me for the cause of truth, and who remained firm to my party, and especially Wenceslaus Duba and John of Chlum, introduced to the Council by the Emperor Sigismund himself.

Having said, that, if I had erred, I should be glad to be instructed of my errors: "Since you desire to be instructed," replied the Grand Cardinal, "you must first of all abjure your doctrine, conformable to the sentence of the fifty doctors and interpreters of the Holy Scriptures." An excellent advice! Therefore, St Catherine should renounce the Word of God and faith in Jesus, because fifty doctors opposed her! But this sublime virgin did not yield; she remained faithful unto death; she thus gained over her judges to Christ; but I cannot in the same manner persuade mine; it is wherefore I have thought fit to write to you, in order you might be informed they have not vanquished me neither by the Scriptures nor by reason, but tried me by terror and by lies to extort an abjuration from me. The God of mercy, whose justice I have glorified, was with me. He is still with me now, and I am confident he will remain with me unto the end.

Written the fourth day after the Festival of John the Baptist, in prison, in chains, and in the expectation of death; and yet I dare not say, on account of the hidden judgment of God, that this letter may be my last; for, even now, the Almighty God may effect my deliverance.

LETTER LI.*

TO HIS FRIENDS.

[He returns them thanks for their kindness.]

May God be with you, and grant you every felicity, for the kindness you have heaped on me. Suffer not the Seignior John,* my best friend, my other self, to expose himself to peril for my sake. I ask this of you, of you, Seignior Peter, in particular, in the name of the Lord. Lastly, I conjure you to live according to God's word, and obey his precepts, as I have taught you to do. Render thanks to his Royal Majesty for all the benefits that I have received from him.

Salute for me your families and my other friends, whom I cannot name here individually. I pray to God for you; pray to him for me, to that great God, near whom, with his aid, we shall all yet arrive. Amen.

I think that I shall have to suffer for the word of God. But you will not, I conjure you in his name, permit his ministers and saints to be rigorously treated.

JOHN HUSS, in hope, servant of God.

* *Hist. et. Monum. Johann. Huss*, Epist. xxiv.
† John of Chlum.

P.S.—Peter,* my very dear friend, keep, in remembrance of me, my fur cloak. Seignior Henry, may you live in health with your wife. I thank you for your kindness: may God heap his riches upon you.

LETTER LII.†

TO JOHN OF CHLUM.

I am greatly rejoiced that the Seignior Wenceslaus desires to take to himself a wife, and to flee from the vanities of the world. It is time he should retrace his steps. He has for a long time travelled kingdoms, played at the lance, wearied his body, spent his fortune, and offended his soul. Let him then renounce such a life, and dwell at home in peace with his wife and servants, there to serve God. It is better, indeed, to serve God without sin, in peace and tranquillity of mind, than to serve any other master amidst great anxieties, and to the peril of our souls. Give these lines to my excellent friend to read.

The Lord still preserves the life of John Huss, and

---

* Peter Maldoniewitz, surnamed the Notary.

† *Hist. et Monum. Johann. Huss*, Epist. xxiii.

will continue to do so, as long as it is his good-will, against the efforts of avaricious, proud, and impious men of this Council, where there are but few (God knows if I exaggerate) who obey his precept.

Written on the Festival of the Holy Apostles Peter and Paul.

JOHN HUSS, in hope, servant of Jesus Christ.

LETTER LIII.*

TO JOHN OF CHLUM.

My very dear benefactor in Jesus Christ,—It is no slight satisfaction to me to be able to write to you. Your letter, dated yesterday, has made me understand, first, how will be unveiled and exposed to the light the iniquity of this perverse assembly, of the great prostitute spoken of in the Apocalypse, with whom, spiritually, the kings of the earth pollute themselves, by quitting the truth of the Lord, in order to assist the lies of antichrist, by seduction, fear, or in the hope of acquiring by this alliance the advantages of the world.

* *Hist. et Monum. Johann. Huss,* Epist. xxii.

I understood, secondly, that the enemies of the truth begin to be alarmed. Thirdly, I recognized the charitable order, the intrepid firmness, with which you confess the truth ; and, lastly, I saw with joy that you wished to put an end to the vanities and laborious servitude of the age, and combat for our Lord Jesus Christ ; to serve whom, is, as St Gregory expresses it, to reign. He who faithfully serves him will be served by him in the celestial realms. He has said, " Blessed is that servant whom his Lord, when he cometh, shall find watching ; verily I say unto you, that he shall make him ruler over all his goods." The kings of this world do not act in this manner towards their servants ; they love them only as long as they are useful and necessary to them. This is not the conduct of Jesus, the King of Glory, who crowned the holy apostles, Peter and Paul, introducing the former into the celestial kingdom by crucifixion, &c., the latter by decapitation ; the first after having been imprisoned four times, and delivered by an angel ; the second after having been beaten thrice with rods, once stoned, often afflicted, and twice shipwrecked, and having lingered two years in prison. Now they no longer suffer anxieties and torments, but enjoy a sweet and unchangeable peace, as well as infinite joy: Peter and Paul reign already with the King of Heaven ; they are already among the angelic choir, they behold the King of kings in his magnificence; no sorrows afflict them, and they are filled with ineffable happiness. May these glorious martyrs, now united to the King of Glory, deign to intercede for us, that, strengthened by their assistance, we may participate in their glory, after having suffered with humility ; since the all-powerful God has declared it is for our welfare that we suffer in this world. Amen.

Written on the Festival of the Holy Apostles Peter and Paul.

If you can, write to me again, I beseech you, in the name of the Lord. I conjure you also to salute most particularly the Queen, my sovereign ; advise her to hold fast to the truth, and not to be scandalised on my account, as if I were a heretic. Salute for me also your wife, whom I conjure you to love in Christ ; for I trust she is amongst the children of God, through observing his commandments.

Salute all the friends of the truth.

LETTER LIV.*

TO MASTER JOHN CHRISTIAN.

[Exhortation.]

Christian, my master and benefactor, keep steadfast in the truth of Christ and in the love of his disciples. Fear not; for the Lord will shortly afford us his protection, and augment the number of his faithful believers. Be always kind to the poor, as thou wert wont; guard thy chastity; flee avarice; hold not several livings, but keep thy church, that the faithful may find refuge in· thee, as in the bosom of a father. O thou, whom I love, salute for me Jacobel, and all the friends of the truth.

Written in irons, and expecting to suffer death.

* *Hist. et Monum. Johann. Huss*, Epist. xvii.

LETTER LV.*

TO HIS BENEFACTORS.

[He exhorts them to prefer serving our Saviour Jesus Christ, who will not deceive them, rather than the princes of the earth.]

My excellent benefactors, I exhort you,† by the bowels of Jesus Christ, you who defend the truth, to renounce the vanities of the age, and to combat for our eternal King, Jesus Christ. Put not your trust in princes, nor in the children of men ; for the children of men are false and full of lies. To-day they live, and to-morrow they are no more : God alone is eternal. He has servants, not for his own wants, but for the advantage even of his servants, on whom he bestows the riches he has promised them ; for he has said—" Where I am, there also shall be my servant." The Lord renders his servants masters of all he possesses, giving himself up to them, and giving all with himself, in order that they may, without weariness, and without anxiety, possess all things and rejoice with all the saints in eternal happiness. *Blessed is*

---

* *Hist. et Monum. Johann. Huss*, Epist. xxi.
† Hortor vos per viscera Jesu Christi.

the servant who watches when his Lord cometh. For-tunate is the servant who shall joyfully repose on the bosom of the King of Glory! Serve, then, this King with fear, you who love him with all your heart. He will conduct you in safety to Bohemia in his grace, and afterwards, I trust, into eternal glory. Adieu; for I believe this let-ter may be the last that I shall write to you; to-morrow I shall be cleansed from my sins by a cruel death, in the hope of Christ. I cannot write what has occurred to me this night. Sigismund has done all with trick and cunning; may God forgive him! . . . . . You have heard the sentence which he delivered. Do not, I conjure you, suspect in the slightest degree the faithful Vitus.

LETTER LVI., AND THE LAST.*

TO HIS FAITHFUL FRIEND LEDERTZ.

Seignior Ledertz, my faithful friend, you, Dame Mar-garet, and all of you who love me, may God bestow on you all his riches, for the great trouble you have taken, and for the many favours that I have received at your hands! Dear and faithful Master Christian, may God

---

* *Hist. et Monum. Johann. Huss,* Epist. **xxv.**

be with you! Master Martin, my disciple, forget not the faithful manner in which I taught you the word of God! Master Nicholas, Peter, the priest of the Lord, the King, the masters and heads of the University, preserve faithfully God's word! May Gallus preach it, and all of you, my beloved, listen attentively to it, and guard it in your hearts!

END OF JOHN HUSS'S LETTERS.

REMARKS ON THE WORKS OF JOHN HUSS.

The writings of JOHN HUSS, which have been handed down to us, may be classed under four principal heads:—His letters; his works and commentaries on the Scriptures; his sermons; and, lastly, his moral and theological treatises. His letters have been given in this volume. His particular works on the Scriptures are,—

1st, A History of the Life of Jesus Christ, according to the Four Gospels.

2dly, The History of our Lord's Passion, as collected from the Four Gospels, and augmented by notes and commentaries from the most celebrated Doctors of the Church.

3dly, The Explanation of the First Seven Chapters of the First Epistle of St Paul to the Corinthians.

4thly, Commentaries on the Seven Canonical Epistles of the Apostles St James, St Peter, St John, and St Jude.

5thly, Explanations and Developments of the Psalms cix., cx., cxi., cxii., cxiii., cxiv., cxv., cxvi., cxvii., and cxviii.

All these writings reveal in their author a profound knowledge of the sacred books, and of the works of the Fathers, as well as a great zeal to diffuse the light of the

Scriptures, and to draw from them salutary instruction.
They indicate, besides, an independence of views which
must have given umbrage to the clergy.   It is thus that
Huss, in arranging the Epistles of the Apostles, names
first that of St James, who, he says, presided at the
Council of Jerusalem.   He assigns the first place to this
Epistle, on account of the superior dignity which the
Apostle bears in the eyes of Christians by reason of
three different claims :—"First, In addressing himself
particularly to converted Jews, who were superior to the
pagans ; afterwards, in consideration of his personal
merit ; for although Peter was the first of the apostles,
nevertheless the first evangelical preaching is traced to
St James ;—and lastly, in consideration of the dignity of
the place where he held his See, which was Jerusalem,
where the first preaching of God's word took place." *

These works of John Huss on the Scriptures, so different in their nature, and so considerable in their extent,
are, however, like most of the theological writings of
the epoch, prolix and diffuse.   The author subdivides
his matter without end, fatigues with his repetitions, and,
in his commentaries, presents, in general, subtile explanations and interpretations, sometimes trifling, and often
forced, in order to discover in each word of the sacred
books of the Old Testament, the type of our Saviour's
words in the New one.

* *Hist. et Monum. Johann. Huss*, t. ii., p. 176.

The sermons and discourses of John Huss, collected in his works, amount to about forty, amongst which several were pronounced before his rupture with his ecclesiastical superiors, and his interdiction.   In them might be already recognised that pure and ardent zeal for morality, and that horror for the vices of the clergy, which animated his bosom in every circumstance of his life—a manifestation at once noble and rash in an age when the clergy were as powerful as they were corrupt, and which accumulated on the head of John Huss such implacable resentment.

In some sermons, delivered at a later period, and when he was already exposed to the attacks of his enemies, he expresses himself openly against the abuses springing from the doctrines of the Roman Church.   He energetically censures the pomp and ostentation displayed in the festivals in honour of the saints.   He reproves the lying flatteries of funeral eulogiums, and the profit derived from them by the priest.   He alludes to this verse—

De morbo medicus gaudet, de morte sacerdos ;*

and adds : " What is the use of multiplying vigils in the house of a rich defunct, unless, indeed, for empty praise ? Neither he who pays, nor he who is paid, care much about the psalms that are sung.   What utility is there in this pompous cortege of the rich at the burial of a corpse ? Why are so many priests sitting luxuriously on

* The physician delights in disease, the priest in death.

cushions round a coffin, whilst thou, O Christ! stoodst weeping over the tomb of Lazarus, and humbly invokedst thy Father? We do not weep, but make merry; we utter not pious groans, but vain clamours."*

John Huss believed in purgatory, although he placed but little confidence in the efficacy of praying for the dead; and in the sermon already mentioned, he supports his opinion on this point by the silence of the Scriptures. " We find no mention made of it," he remarks, " except in the Book of Maccabees, which is not placed by the Jews in the canon of the Old Testament; neither the prophets, nor Jesus Christ, nor the Apostles, nor the saints who have followed their footsteps, have explicitly taught that the dead should be prayed for; but they have publicly declared, that whoever lived without crime should be deemed holy. For my part, I think that the introduction of this custom originated in the avarice of the priests, who, though but little desirous of teaching men to live well after the examples of the prophets, of Christ and the Apostles, carefully exhort them to make rich offerings, in the hope of procuring celestial happiness, and a speedy deliverance from purgatory."†

The first nine sermons collected in the works of John Huss ‡ were preached by him in Prague at different

* *Hist. et Monum. Johann. Huss.* Sermo habitus Pragæ in Synodo ad Clerum, t. ii., p. 77.

† Ubi supra, p. 82.

‡ *Hist. et Monum. Johann. Huss,* t. ii.

periods, and are followed by twenty-eight discourses relative to *Antichrist*, in which he openly designates the Pope, and where he repeats most of the arguments of the treatise, *On the Anatomy of the Members of Antichrist*.

The last two sermons of John Huss are those which he composed on arriving at Constance ; the one on *Faith*, the other on *Peace*. They breathe the desire of a reconciliation, which his enemies repulsed, and he was not permitted to deliver them.

The moral and theological treatises form the fourth part of John Huss's works, and the most important of the whole, for they especially shew his doctrines, and were those which furnished his enemies and judges with arguments and arms against him.*

The principal of the treatises are :—*The Treatise on the Church*, publicly read in the city of Prague ; *The Refutation of the Bull of John XXIII., concerning Indulgences for the First Crusade ;†   Answer to Stephen Paletz ; Answer to Stanislas Zuöima ; Refutation of the Writing of Eight Doctors of Prague ; The Book of Antichrist;* and the *Treatise on the Abominations of Priests and Monks*.

All the doctrines and peculiar opinions of John Huss are to be met with in his celebrated *Treatise on the Church,*

---

* For the complete list of John Huss's treatises, see Note B.

† For this celebrated writing, consult *Reformers before the Reformation*, vol. i., b. i.

and in his *Answers to Paletz, to Stanislas de Znöima,* and *The Eight Doctors.*   It may be discovered, on perusing them, that on a great number of points, which, a century later, separated the Reformers from the Roman Catholic Church, Huss shared the opinion of the latter, or at least did not believe that it was allowable to oppose it ; he attacked it, consequently, much more for its abuses than for its errors.

The horror which he felt at the sight of evil, and especially when it was committed by men who ought to set an example of every virtue to others, often carried him too far.   Anger mingled its violence with his indignation, and, in some treatises, amongst others *The Antichrist,* and *The Abominations of Priests and Monks,* he forgets himself so far as to indulge in abuse, and employ insulting and offensive expressions.   Nevertheless, it would be unjust to see, on that account, an excuse for those who condemned him ; for these treatises were not known to them, and were only made public after his death.   Besides, the expressions to be blamed in them belong less to John Huss than to the age in which he lived.   They are to be met with in the writings of the most celebrated Doctors and orthodox priests ; and it seems that, in hazarding a language which astonishes our more sensitive ears, John Huss had adopted for his authority the Prophet Ezekiel, from whom he often drew his inspirations.

Among the doctrines signalized as heretical in the works of Huss are those on *Predestination* and *Election.* A heresy was seen in the definition which Huss gives of the Catholic and the universal Church, " *This Church,*" says he, " *is the assembly of all the elect, present, past, and future, including also the angels.*"* And lower down he adds :—" *No particular tie, no human election, renders a person member of the universal Church, but divine predestination alone ; this predestination is, according to St Augustin, election by the grace of the Divine will, or preparation to grace in the present life, and to glory in the future one.*"†

To these different passages has been opposed the necessity of the sacraments for obtaining salvation ; and it has thence been concluded, that, whoever admitted predestination, gratuitous safety of election and grace, or communion with the universal Church—could attribute no efficacy to the sacraments—to the communion of the external and visible Church.‡   Nevertheless, Huss nowhere disputes the virtue of the sacraments, but, on the contrary, recommends their frequent use. ˙This doctrine of *predestination* and *election* has often divided the Catholic Church.   It has been supported in every age by some of its most illustrious members, and has had for in-

---

* *De Eccles.*   † Ibid.
‡ Retrum Hussi doctrina fuerit hæresies.   *Dissert. Hist. Dogmat.* *Coppenberg.*

terpreters St Augustin and Gerson.* The boldest opinions of John Huss have almost all of them found partizans among men whom Rome venerates as saints and learned doctors. But he separated from them upon two principal points : in his eyes, as in those of Wycliffe, the authority of the Church could only direct the faith and conduct, as long as the decisions of the Church agreed with the Scriptures ; and the priest, whatever his external dignity might be, was not, in the sight of God, priest, bishop, or pope, and representative of Jesus Christ, but as far as he took for model and guide in his private life the example of our Saviour. These two capital points, on which repose all the doctrine of Wycliffe, are the real basis of all Christian dissent. Huss, as we stated in a previous work, acknowledged them without calculating their importance, without clearly understanding the abyss they opened between him and the Church of which he believed himself a member. His opinion on this subject strongly manifests itself in all the above-mentioned treatises. Even his adversaries are forced to admit that he derived it from the unshaken conviction that morality and religion are inseparable, and that they who have the mission of representing Jesus on earth could not desire or order otherwise than what God himself had willed and commanded.

On these two points, he goes beyond the limits of the

---

* Gers. Oper. *De Conosolat. Theolog.*, t. i. p. 137.

Roman Church, and openly subjects himself to the reproach addressed to him by one of the Catholic writers, who judged him most impartially. " It is greatly to be lamented," says the writer alluded to, " that such a man should have so frightful a destiny, and so bitter a death, —he, who. glowed with so ardent a love for Christ and his doctrine,—who shone, by the integrity of his life, the sincerity of his heart, the ardour of his mind, his eloquence, and other precious gifts, to so high a degree, that he might have become an illustrious Reformer, if, after the example of some very eminent men, such as Gerson, d'Ailly, or Clémangis, he had devoted his talents to the work of reform in the Church itself, and not out of its bosom." *

This reproach is best refuted by referring to John Huss's life, and the history of his time. Both form the subject of the work, which this one completes, and to which the reader has been often referred.† It will be there seen that the reform of abuses could not be accomplished by

* Maxime quidem dolendum esse ingenue confitemur quod tristissimam sortem necemque acerbissimam vir ille perpessus est, qui magno exarsit Christi reique christianæ amore, vitæ integritate voluntate sincera, maximo animi ardore, præstantissima concionaudi facultate aliisque virtutibus mire excelluit, ita ut reformator extitisset egregius si cum æqualibus viris præclarissimis, Gersonio, Petro ab Alliaco, Nicolao Clemangis ea qua potuit ac debuit ratione intra, non extra Ecclesiæ fines, reformandæ Ecclesiæ operam novasset. *Dissert. hist. dogmat.* Cappenberg.

† *The Reformers before the Reformation.*

those whose interests it was to perpetuate them, and that the corruption of the external and visible Church was then so profound, that to introduce a reform in it, it was necessary first to leave it altogether.

———

Of all John Huss's treatises, that on *The Church* is the most complete and celebrated. We must insert here an analysis of it, which will terminate this work.

ANALYSIS OF THE TREATISE ON THE CHURCH.

John Huss defines the universal Church to be the assembly of all the predestined, past, present, and to come, including the angels. " The Church," writes he, " is the most excellent thing created by God. We ought not therefore to believe in the Church, because it is not God; but we should believe that there is a holy univer- sal Church, of which Jesus Christ is the sole Chief. The entire Church and all its parts ought to honour God ; but it ought not to wish that divine worship should be rendered her." *

" Reprobates," says Huss, " are not members of the

* Tota ecclesia et quælibet ejus pars debet Deum colere et nec ipsa nec ejus pars sult coli pro deo.—*De Eccles. J. Huss, Hist. et Monum.*, t. i., p. 244.

Church. It may occur that one is in the Church, without being of the Church. Such may be the case with the popes, bishops, priests, and clergy, although they style themselves the Church in particular, because it is possible that they are reprobate: we may also belong to the Church, without being exteriorly in the Church, like those who commence to be converted to the faith."

Huss next examines the celebrated passage of St Matthew: *Thou art Peter, and on this rock will I build my Church, and the gates of hell shall not prevail against it; and I will give thee the keys of the kingdom of heaven, &c.* (Matthew xvi., 18, 19). He considers in it four things: *The Church*, its *faith*, its *foundation*, and its *power*. He examines, first of all, whether the Roman Church is the universal one, as is affirmed by the canon law, where the Pope is called the chief, and the cardinals, the body of the Church. He denies this to be the case, for the reason that the Pope and the cardinals do not compose the whole assembly of the elect. *Thou art Peter, and on this rock will I build my Church*, signifies, according to Huss, " Thou art the confessor of the true Rock, which is Christ; and it is on this rock that I will raise my Church by faith and by grace; but this Church does not consist in men, constituted in power and dignities, whether secular or ecclesiastical, because several popes have fallen into error and crime."

Huss does not, however, contest great privileges to the Roman Church, because St Peter founded it; and he does not oppose the Pope and the cardinals holding the principal rank in the Church, provided they follow the example of Jesus Christ, and that, stripping themselves of pomp and ambition, they serve with humility the common mother of all believers.

Yet the Roman Church can hardly be termed a universal one, because, in reality, it is a particular Church; the first and most ancient being that of Jerusalem, and the second that of Antioch, of which the faithful were the first called Christians.*

As to faith, Huss distinguishes several kinds. " The true faith," says he, "is faith formed by charity.† This, when persevered in, is the foundation of all the other Christian virtues; it ought necessarily to be founded on *truth*, which enlightens the understanding, and on *authority*, which strengthens the soul. This authority can be only that of God speaking by his word. If the Christian is convinced that a truth has been dictated by the Holy Ghost in the Scriptures, he ought, without hesitation, to declare his opinion, and expose his life for it. The obli-

---

* *De Eccles.*, p. 258. Compare this opinion with that of Gerson on the same subject. *Gers. Opera*, v. 11.—*De modis uniendi ac reform. Eccles. en Concil.* See also the *Reformers before the Reformation*, Introduction, sect. v.

† Unde quicumque habuerit fidem charitate firmatam in communis sufficit cum virtute perseverantiæ, ad salutem.

gation is not the same with regard to the words of the saints, and popes' bulls : one is not held to believe them, but only so far as they agree with the Holy Scriptures. We may, besides, believe in them as in opinions, because the Pope and his court might err, through ignorance of the truth. It is, then, one thing to believe in God, because he cannot err or be deceived, and another to believe in the Pope, who is liable to error; it is one thing to believe the Holy Scriptures, and another to believe in a bull, because the latter is of human invention. It can never be permitted not to follow the Scriptures, or to oppose them ; but it is sometimes allowable not to believe in a bull, and even to oppose it, as, for instance, when it has originated in avarice, when it raises to dignity unworthy persons, or oppresses the innocent ; in a word, when it is contrary to the instructions and commandments of God.* As regards the foundation of the Church, there is but one, which is Jesus Christ. If the Apostles, therefore, are called the foundations of the Church, it is in a figurative manner, as being subjected to Jesus Christ, because it is he who has built the Church, and St Peter is only its basis and foundation ; in the same manner is the Apostles his colleagues. It must be admitted, that Jesus Christ, who is the corner-stone of the Church,

---

* The doctrine of the Gallic Church is still more restrictive. It only acknowledges bulls when they are not contrary to the laws of the kingdom.

established Peter in humility, poverty, and faith, and
that it was by these virtues he elevated the Church which
he governed. But to pretend, from these words, *On this
rock will I raise my Church*, that Jesus Christ intended
to found the entire Church in the person of *Peter*, is to
believe what is contrary to faith and reason. St Peter
never boasted of being the head of the whole Church, because he never governed the whole of it ; yet there may
be allowed to him, with some of the Fathers, a priority
of order over the other Apostles, on account of the ex-
cellence of his virtues ; and, *in this sense*, the words of
the blessed St Denis are true : St Peter was the Chief of
the Apostles,* which does not mean the Chief of the
Universal Church.   The Bishop of Rome may be looked
upon as the vicar of St Peter, and the first in the church
which he governs, if he imitate the virtues of this
Apostle ; but if he follow an opposite path, he is only
the forerunner of Antichrist."   Huss supports his opinion by citing several of the Fathers, and amongst others,
St Bernard, St Jerome, St Gregory, and St Chrysostom.
" It is not the post which he holds that makes the priest,"
says the last named saint, " but the priest which makes
the post ; it is not the place which sanctifies man, but
man that sanctifies the place."

" *Lastly*, As relates to the power of priests, it is purely

---

* Et dictum beati Dionysii est verum, quod Petrus fuit capitaneus
inter apostolos. *De Eccles.*, cap. ix.

spiritual; it consists in instructing, in condemning the culpable by spiritual punishment, in absolving the penitent, and announcing to them the remission of their sins; it dwells actually in Jesus Christ, and has been given, in the person of Peter, to all the Church militant.

" Priests are only the ministers of the Church, and are not able to bind or loose, remit or retain sins, if God has not previously done so; and the people greatly err, if they believe that the priests first bind or unbind, and that God only does so after them; as if God executed the sentence of priests, whereas, priests ought to execute the judgment of God, only in accord with Jesus Christ.*

" There are two kinds of power: one legitimate, and which should be obeyed; the other pretended and usurped, which ought to be resisted. Such is the power of Simoniacs, who, through interest, take advantage of the keys in order to condemn the innocent and absolve the guilty; who buy and sell holy orders, bishopricks, canonries, and livings; who make a traffic of the sacraments; who live in avarice and voluptuousness, and sully the authority of the priesthood." Huss maintains that the power of binding or loosing was equally given to all the Apostles, and contests the right of the popes to bear the title of *universal bishop* and *most holy.* " They have no right," he says, " to decorate themselves with it;" and he

---

* *De Eccles.*, cap. x. Compare this opinion of John Huss with that of Wycliffe and Gerson on the same matter, *Reformers before the Reformation.*

cites, as proofs, the example of the Apostles, the canons, the councils, as well as the scandalous lives of several popes, in whom there was no holiness. "As to the cardinals, of whom it is said that they form the body of the Church, it would be necessary, in order to acknow-ledge it, to know by revelation that they are predestined to salvation, and that they live as becomes the successors and vicars of the Apostles; but do they shew themselves as such? Those men who accumulate livings, gain favours by presents after the example of Giezi; who go early in the morning, dressed in splendid clothing, to visit the Pope, mounted on horses richly caparisoned, not on ac-count of the distance or difficulty of the roads, but to display their magnificence to the eyes of the world, in op-position to the example of Christ and his Apostles, who visited on foot, and in humble clothing, the towns and villages, preaching the Gospel, and announcing the king-dom of God.*

"The Church," says John Huss, "may be governed with-out the Pope and cardinals, as was the case during three hundred years. It was Constantine who established, in the third century, the universal domination of the Roman Pontiff. Before the donation, the Bishop of Rome was like the other bishops;† and for that reason, the Roman

* *De Eccles.*, cap. xv.

† This illegality of the donation of Constantine was not then dis-covered.

pontiffs who succeeded Sylvester, fearing to lose this pre-eminence, besought the Emperors to confirm it." John Huss afterwards quotes Gratian's decree, confirmed by Lewis-le-Debonnaire, and adds—" St Peter never required that Lewis-le-Debonnaire should bestow on him the temporal domain of Rome ; he was in possession of the kingdom of heaven, and consequently greater than Lewis. Would to God that Peter had replied to him, I accept not your concession. When I was Bishop of Rome, I did not envy Nero the domination of Rome, and I had no need of it. I believe it to have been injurious to my successors ; it turned them from the preaching of the Gospel, from prayer, and observing the commandments of God, and filled them with pride."

" It is the law of God, and not the arbitrary will of the Pope and cardinals, that ought to regulate ecclesiastical judgment." The adversaries of Huss considered this proposition of his as a crime. He defends it against them, and makes it a point of honour to acknowledge only the Scriptures as authority, although he respects the holy doctors, when their decisions are in harmony with the Divine word. He rejects the application to Christians of certain passages of Deuteronomy, in which God orders the Israelites to have their disputes judged in the place he had chosen, and sentences with death whoever should not submit himself to the Pontiff and to the judge.* " It

* Deut. xvii.

is here a question," says John Huss, "of civil affairs rather than of religious ones, and the spirit of the Gospel, which, only employing persuasion, differs greatly from the ancient law, which was one of rigour.   If these distinctions were not established, it would follow that Jesus was justly condemned, because the high priests Annas and Caiaphas presided in the places designed by God himself."

Huss likewise rejects the accusation of wishing to excite the people, and induce them to disobedience towards their superiors, viz., the pope, bishops, priests, and all the clergy.   He distinguishes three kinds of obedience : 1st, Spiritual obedience, which is that which all Christians, without exception, are expected at all times to render to the law of Jesus Christ.   2dly, Secular obedience, which is that which is due to civil laws, admitting them to be conformable to the law of God.   3dly, Ecclesiastical obedience, which is that paid to the laws invented by the priests of the Church without any express authority of the Scriptures.   "This latter," he says, "is only obligatory as far as the things prescribed or forbidden are in conformity with what is ordered or prohibited by the Word of God;" and he draws this inference, "*that he who knows of a certainty that the commandments of the Pope are contrary to what is counselled and commanded by Jesus Christ, or tends to the ruin of the Church, ought boldly to resist them, for fear of sanctioning a crime by his consent.*"   He invokes, in support of this opinion the authority of the canon law, as well as the Fathers, from whom he quotes many passages, extracted especially from Nicholas Lyra and Saint Augustin.* In the last chapters, Huss inveighs energetically against the abuse of *excommunication, suspensions,* and *interdicts.*

" One ought not to be excommunicated," continues Huss, " but on account of a mortal sin which separates from the grace of God. The *major excommunication* is pronounced against a public sinner, and it is that which was pronounced against myself; but blessed be God, who has not given to this excommunication the power of taking away justice and virtue from a just man, and of making him become a sinner. . . . I am more afraid of the greatest of all excommunications, viz. that by which the Sovereign Pontiff, in presence of angels and men, will eternally excommunicate the wicked from all participation in eternal beatitude. . . . It is on that One, that he who judges should reflect, through fear of excommunicating unjustly; for whoever shall excommunicate a man from temporal interest or pride, or in order to revenge himself of some injury, and against his conscience, excommunicates himself.†

" As to suspension, it is God who pronounces it against every bad priest who lives scandalously and criminally.

---

* Consult on this subject, and compare with this passage, Letter V. of the First Series, pages 24–29.

† *De Eccles.,* cap. xxii.

It follows from hence, that there are but few preachers whom God does not at present suspend from the ministry of his Word, because there are few who do not reject the knowledge of the Scriptures, and contradict, by their lives, the duties which they teach unto others." Huss concludes from this, that he was forced to preach against the vices of the clergy. " Wo unto me," he exclaims, " if I had remained silent; for, according to the canon law,* not to oppose an error is to approve of it; and to neglect denouncing the perverse when it is in our power to do so, is to shew ourselves their accomplices.†"

Afterwards passing to the subject of interdicts, a punishment which ecclesiastical dignitaries may inflict on a country or town, simply for the fault of one individual, and forbidding divine service to be celebrated in the place, without distinguishing the innocent from the guilty, John Huss adds : " One of the manifest proofs that these censures, which are called *fulminations*, are derived from Antichrist, is, that they are cast against those who preach the Gospel, and expose the corruption of the clergy. Interdicts began after the year one thousand, and by the rage of Satan, when the clergy had become fat on the misfortunes of the world, and had grown in voluptuousness, pride, and impatience of submitting to any restraint."

Huss calls to mind the worldly motives which led the

---

* Distinct. 83.

† Error cui non resistitur approbatur.

pontiffs, Adrian IV., Alexander III., Innocent III., Boniface VIII., Innocent IV., and Clement IV., to interdict towns and countries, in the thirteenth and fourteenth centuries, and concludes by quoting, against this custom, an admirable letter of St Augustin to a young bishop, who, on account of the ill-conduct of a holy father, had excommunicated his whole family.   This is the letter :—
" Instruct me, I pray you, by strict reason or Scripture, in what case, should you know of any, the child should be excommunicated for the sin of the father, the wife for that of the husband, the servant for the master, and even the children that may be born in the house thus excommunicated, since, as long as it remains so, it is impossible to procure for the children, even when in danger of death, the grace of regeneration produced by Baptism. The chastisement which God inflicted on several of the impious who had despised his law, and in which he included all belonging to them, was an external punishment, which fell only on the body, in order to fill the living with dread ; but the excommunication resulting from the power given us by these words : ' *That which you shall have bound on earth, shall be bound in heaven,*' falls even upon the soul ; and it is said of souls : ' The soul of the father belongs to me, as likewise the soul of the son ; and that which has sinned shall die.'   Perhaps you have heard of some bishops of great repute, who anathemised sinners with the whole of their families ; but if they were

asked to explain their conduct, it is likely they would be embarrassed to assign a good reason for it; and as I should not myself have known how to answer a similar inquiry, I have never, on that account, dared to act in this manner, however great might have been the crimes committed against the Church. Nevertheless, if God has revealed to you that this may be done with justice, I shall not despise your youth, and your little experience of the weight of episcopacy. Behold me, then, an old man, and for many years a bishop, ready to learn from a young man, my colleague a year since only, how I should justify myself before God and men, if I inflicted a spiritual punishment on innocent souls for the sins of others."*

John Huss, after supporting his argument by the imposing authority of St Augustin, energetically addresses the doctors, his adversaries, and asks them if they believe in their conscience that it is an unimportant thing, keeping the middle path between good and evil, to deprive the innocent of the sacraments, and of sepulture —to prohibit divine service, and give rise, in consequence, to so much scandal, calumny, and hatred. " O doctors !" he exclaims, " to what church belongs this language ? Is it that of an apostolical church ? Say whether it be the language of an apostle, or of a saint. Assuredly it is not that of Jesus Christ, of the Chief of the Holy Church,

* _De Eccles._, cap. xxiii.

in whose word is contained every truth useful to the Church."*

Huss terminates his celebrated treatise by alluding to the condemnation of the forty-five articles of Wycliffe, by the doctors, without their being able to demonstrate that any of these articles were heretical, erroneous, or scandalous.   He expresses his astonishment at his adversaries abstaining from opposing too openly, at Prague, Wycliffe's proposition, which authorizes lay lords to strip of their wealth ecclesiastics of depraved morals.   " They are silent," says he, " like the priests and Pharisees, and fear prevents them from condemning this article ; but what they dreaded has occurred, and will again come to pass. *They shall lose their temporal wealth ; God grant they may preserve their souls !"*

* O doctores, cujus ecclesiæ est ille stylus ? Numquam apostolicæ ? Dicite cujus apostoli est stylus ille, vel cujus sancti post apostolos ? Numquam est Christi stylus, illius capitis Ecclesiæ sanctæ, in cujus stylo omnis veritas utilis Ecclesiæ est contenta.   Cap. xxiii.

FINIS.

NOTES.

PREFACE OF MARTIN LUTHER TO THE FOUR LETTERS OF JOHN HUSS,
WHICH HE CAUSED TO BE TRANSLATED INTO LATIN, AND WHICH
HE PUBLISHED SEPARATELY AT WIRTEMBERG, IN THE YEAR 1536.

Of these four Letters, written by John Huss in the Bohemian tongue,
I have procured a Latin translation, with the view of publishing them
forthwith, in the same year fixed for a General Council, at the earnest
request of our illustrious Emperor Charles. I have not taken this
trouble with the view of calling down indignation and contempt upon
the Council of Constance. This, on account of its culpable acts, I have
done elsewhere, and will always be ready to do, in defence of the interests of the whole Church. My motive in publishing these Letters,
is, if God permits the said Council to assemble, to warn the members to
take care not to follow the example of the Council of Constance, in
which the Truth was exposed to such lengthened and violent attacks; and yet, nevertheless, now triumphs, and, raising its victorious
head, shews this unworthy assembly in its naked aspect, and stripped
of its tyrannical authority. In this Council, indeed, the cardinals
and most distinguished men aimed principally at extinguishing schism;
they abandoned the cause of religion as below their notice, and left it
to the perverse race of monks and sophists; from whence has sprung,
as formerly from Babylon, all the evil which has produced, in Germany and in Bohemia, so many calamities, wars, massacres, and inex-
tinguishable hatreds. The Papacy, freed from schism, did not afterwards behave less cruelly towards the world, filling the churches with
false doctrines, indulgences, mercenary masses, and all sorts of inventions of priests and monks. Such are the fruits of this sacred Council; it would, therefore, be dangerous to trust again, at this time, the

K

interests of religion to the rage of these perverse men ; but it is of consequence that kings, princes, and bishops, combine all their energies, in order that similar calamities, and more frightful ones, be not the result of the new Council now summoned.

Certainly God has sufficiently shewn, in the Council of Constance, how he resists the proud, how he confounds the lofty in their own designs, without regard to the external dignity of any one.

I publish, therefore, these Letters with the design of giving salutary warning. He who, having been thus warned, will not listen to advice, will perish dreadfully, but not through my fault. May Jesus Christ give us the spirit of prayer, and grant to those who are called to direct this Council, to seek first the things which are of God, and to neglect and undervalue those which concern themselves.

Note B., p. 197.

TREATISES OF JOHN HUSS, ACCORDING TO THE ORDER OF THEIR DATES.

1°. Treatise on the Glorified Blood of Jesus Christ.*

2°. Treatise on the Books of Heretics which should be read and not burned.

3°. Answer to the Englishman John Stokes, the Calmuniator of Wycliffe.

4°. Vindication of some of the Articles of Wycliffe.

5°. On the Withdrawal of Temporal Goods from the Clergy.

6°. On Tithes.

7°. On the Crusade published by Pope John XXIII. against Ladislaus.

8°. Refutation of the Bull of John XXIII. touching the Indulgences for that Crusade.

9°. Answer to an Unknown Adversary.

10°. Answer to the Preacher in Plzna.

---

* This Treatise, approved of by the Archbishop Sbinks, is as early as the year 1404 or 1405. It was written before John Huss had been denounced or persecuted by the clergy.

11°. Of the Five Duties of a Priest.

12°. On the question of knowing whether it be allowable publicly to denounce the Views of the Clergy.

13°. Researches upon Three Doubts, namely, Whether we must believe in the Pope? Whether it be possible to be saved without Confession to a Priest? and whether any learned Doctor has said that any of those overtaken with Pharaoh, or destroyed with Sodom, can be saved?

14°. On what we must Believe?

15°. Treatise on the Six Errors received in the Church.

16°. Answer to Stephen Paletz.

17°. Answer to Stanislaus by Znöima.

18°. Refutation of the Writings of Eight Doctors of Theology.

19°. Treatise of the Church.

20°. The Book of Antichrist.—Anatomy of its Members.

21°. Of the Reign, the Life, and the Manners of Antichrist.

22°. Of the Abomination of Priests and Monks in the Church of Jesus Christ.

TREATISES WRITTEN BY JOHN HUSS IN HIS PRISON, FOR THE EDIFICATION OF HIS KEEPERS.

1°. Explanation of the Apostles' Creed, of the Decalogue, and of the Lord's Prayer.

2°. Of Mortal Sins.

3°. Of Marriage.

4°. Of the Knowledge and Love of God.

5°. Of the Three Enemies of Man.

6°. Of the Seven Mortal Sins.

7°. Of Penitence.

8°. Of the Sacrament of the Body and Blood of Christ.

TREATISES OMITTED IN THE FIRST EDITION OF THE WORKS OF JOHN
HUSS, THE DATES OF WHICH ARE UNKNOWN.

1°. Against the Opinion that the Body of Christ is Created in the
Sacrament of the Altar.

2°. Against the Worshipping of Images.

3°. Of the Abolition of Sects and Human Traditions.

4°. Of Schism and the Unity of the Church.

5°. Of Evangelical Perfection.

6°. A Fragment on the Mystery of Iniquity.

7°. A Fragment on the Revelation of Christ and Antichrist.

8°. Fragments on Diverse Subjects.

PRINTED BY NEILL AND COMPANY, EDINBURGH.

FOURTH THOUSAND.
Just Published, in 18mo, price 1s. 6d. cloth,

ELEMENTS OF SACRED TRUTH FOR THE YOUNG.
By JOHN ABERCROMBIE, M.D.,
Fellow of the Royal College of Physicians, Edinburgh, &c.

PART I.

" The learned Doctor has fulfilled his self-imposed task in a manner which reflects great credit upon him; and his little work can hardly fail to be extensively useful, since it is lucidly written, simple in its arrangement, and pervaded with a warm current of mingled piety and philanthropy."—*Derbyshire Courier.*

" This little book, intended chiefly for the young, is marked with that clearness and depth of reasoning which characterize all the writings of the late Dr Abercrombie. Nor is the pious feeling with which the work is imbued less worthy of attention. As a publication likely to be eminently beneficial, we heartily recommend it."—*The Atlas.*

By the same Author,
In one volume 18mo, price 3s. 6d. cloth, or elegantly bound in morocco, price 6s.,

ESSAYS AND TRACTS;
CONSISTING OF

I.—Culture and Discipline of the Mind. II.—Harmony of Christian Faith and Character. III.—Think on These Things. IV.—The Contest and the Armour. V.—The Messiah as an Example.

Also, to be had separately,
Twenty-Third Thousand, in 18mo, price 1s.,

THE CULTURE AND DISCIPLINE OF THE MIND:
ADDRESSED TO THE YOUNG.

" We by no means overrate the merits of this Address when we say, that no parent or guardian could render a more useful service to the young engaged in liberal studies, than to put a copy of this earnest, impressive, and most judicious Address into their hands."—*Christian Instructor.*

Twenty-Third Thousand, in 18mo, price 1s. 6d.,

THE HARMONY OF CHRISTIAN FAITH AND CHRISTIAN CHARACTER.

" These tracts, as proceeding from an elder of our Church, reflect the highest honour on Dr Abercrombie. It is beautiful to see an individual of his professional celebrity thus coming out of his sphere, and dedicating his talents and a portion of his time to the religious instruction of the poor. Such an example is above all praise."—*Christian Instructor.*

THINK ON THESE THINGS.
Twenty-Third Thousand, price 6d.

THE MESSIAH AS AN EXAMPLE.
Sixth Thousand, price 8d.

THE CONTEST AND THE ARMOUR.
Seventh Thousand, price 8d.

Published this day, in 12mo, handsomely bound in cloth, 5s.,
or if in extra cloth, gilt edges, 5s. 6d.,

JANE BOUVERIE; OR, PROSPERITY AND ADVERSITY.

By CATHERINE SINCLAIR,

Author of " Modern Accomplishments," " Modern Society," " Scotland
and the Scotch," " Hill and Valley," " Holiday House,"
" Charles Seymour," &c. &c.

—

" Still to ourselves in every place consign'd,
Our own felicity we make or find."—*Goldsmith.*

—

" We take leave of Jane Bouverie, and recommend her affecting autobiography
to all who admire the feminine loveliness of a good and graceful woman,
sketched without exaggeration, without formality, and simply as represented in
the portraiture of every-day life."—*Edinburgh Advertiser.*

" There is, as in the other popular works of this clever authoress, much
knowledge of character and of the human heart."—*The Torch.*

Of whom may be had all of Miss Sinclair's other Works.

Published, in One Volume 12mo, Fifth Edition,
price 7s. 6d.,

LETTERS, CHIEFLY PRACTICAL AND CONSOLATORY;

Designed to Illustrate the Nature and Tendency of the Gospel.

By DAVID RUSSELL, D.D., Dundee.

" These letters exhibit the full development of a mind highly gifted with the
power of correct discrimination, richly imbued with the spirit of pure and vital
Christianity ; and familiarised to comprehensive and connected views of scrip-
tural truths in all their mutual relations and practical bearings."—*Eclectic Re-
view.*

Published, in post 8vo, Fourth Edition,
price 7s. 6d. cloth,

MEMOIR OF MRS MARGARET WILSON, OF THE SCOTTISH MISSION, BOMBAY.

Including Extracts from her Letters and Journals.

By JOHN WILSON, D.D., M.R.A.S.,

Honorary President of the Bombay Branch of the Royal Asiatic Society,
and Missionary of the Free Church of Scotland, Bombay.

Published, in post 8vo, Second Edition, price 5s. 6d. cloth,

SERMONS ON PRACTICAL SUBJECTS.

By DAVID WELSH, D.D., F.R.S.E.

Professor of Divinity and Church History, New College, Edinburgh ;
formerly Regius Professor of Divinity and Church History
in the University of Edinburgh.

" We have seldom perused a volume of Discourses in every respect so excellent as this. Characterised by profound thought, luminous arrangement, and
philosophical precision, they are fitted to instruct the most intelligent, whilst
they possess the rare but invaluable charm of perfect simplicity in arrangement
and style."—*Glasgow Courier.*

TREATISES ON THE LORD'S SUPPER.

In 12mo, price 2s. cloth,

THE COMMUNICANT'S COMPANION;

Or, Instruction for the Right Receiving of the LORD'S SUPPER.

By the REV. MATTHEW HENRY.

With an Introductory Essay,
By the REV. JOHN BROWN, D.D., Edinburgh.

In 12mo, price 3s. cloth,

SACRAMENTAL MEDITATIONS AND ADVICES.

By the REV. JOHN WILLISON,
Late Minister of the Gospel at Dundee.

New Edition, in 12mo, price 3s. cloth,

A CATECHISM ON THE NATURE AND USES OF THE LORD'S SUPPER.

By the REV. JOHN WILLISON,
Late Minister of the Gospel at Dundee.

In 18mo, Fourth Edition, price 1s. 6d. cloth,

FOUR ADDRESSES ON SUBJECTS CONNECTED WITH THE LORD'S SUPPER.

By CHARLES WATSON, D.D.
Late Minister of Burntisland.

In 18mo, Fifteenth Edition, price 1s. 6d. cloth,

SACRAMENTAL EXERCISES.

By JABEZ EARLE, D.D.

With an Introductory Essay,
By ANDREW THOMSON, D.D.,
Late Minister of St George's Church, Edinburgh.

In 18mo, price 3d. stitched,

A CATECHISM FOR THE INSTRUCTION OF COMMUNICANTS IN THE NATURE AND USES OF THE LORD'S SUPPER.

And in the Doctrines and Duties connected with that Ordinance.

By ANDREW THOMSON, D.D.,
Late Minister of St George's Church, Edinburgh.

CPSIA information can be obtained
at www.ICGtesting.com
Printed in the USA
BVHW01s2147180118
505739BV00019B/228/P